Two Minds of a Western Poet

## POETS ON POETRY

**Annie Finch and Marilyn Hacker, General Editors**
**Donald Hall, Founding Editor**

*New titles*

Kazim Ali, *Orange Alert*
Martín Espada, *The Lover of a Subversive Is Also a Subversive*
Marilyn Hacker, *Unauthorized Voices*
David Mason, *Two Minds of a Western Poet*

*Recently published*

Meena Alexander, *Poetics of Dislocation*
Annie Finch, *The Body of Poetry*
Sandra M. Gilbert, *On Burning Ground: Thirty Years of
    Thinking About Poetry*
Grace Schulman, *First Loves and Other Adventures*
Reginald Shepherd, *Orpheus in the Bronx*
Reginald Shepherd, *A Martian Muse: Further Essays on
    Identity, Politics, and the Freedom of Poetry*

*Also available, collections by*

Elizabeth Alexander, A. R. Ammons, John Ashbery, Robert Bly,
Philip Booth, Marianne Boruch, Hayden Carruth, Amy Clampitt,
Alfred Corn, Douglas Crase, Robert Creeley, Donald Davie,
Thomas M. Disch, Ed Dorn, Tess Gallagher, Dana Gioia,
Linda Gregerson, Allen Grossman, Thom Gunn, Rachel Hadas,
John Haines, Donald Hall, Joy Harjo, Robert Hayden, Edward Hirsch,
Daniel Hoffman, Jonathan Holden, John Hollander, Paul Hoover,
Andrew Hudgins, Laura (Riding) Jackson, Josephine Jacobsen,
Mark Jarman, Galway Kinnell, Kenneth Koch, John Koethe,
Yusef Komunyakaa, Maxine Kumin, Martin Lammon (editor),
Philip Larkin, David Lehman, Philip Levine, Larry Levis, John Logan,
William Logan, William Matthews, William Meredith, Jane Miller,
David Mura, Carol Muske, Alice Notley, Geoffrey O'Brien, Gregory Orr,
Alicia Suskin Ostriker, Ron Padgett, Marge Piercy, Anne Sexton,
Karl Shapiro, Charles Simic, William Stafford, Anne Stevenson,
May Swenson, James Tate, Richard Tillinghast, C. K. Williams,
Alan Williamson, Charles Wright, James Wright, John Yau, and
Stephen Yenser

*David Mason*

# Two Minds of a Western Poet

ESSAYS

THE UNIVERSITY OF MICHIGAN PRESS
*Ann Arbor*

2014   2013   2012   2011     4   3   2   1

*A CIP catalog record for this book is available from the British Library.*

Library of Congress Cataloging-in-Publication Data

Mason, David (David James), 1954–
    Two minds of a western poet : essays / by David Mason.
        p. cm. — (Poets on poetry)
    ISBN 978-0-472-07142-5 (acid-free paper) — ISBN 978-0-472-
05142-7 (pbk. : acid-free paper)
    1. Mason, David (David James), 1954–   2. American poetry—
20th century—History and criticism.   3. American poetry—West
(U.S.)—History and criticism.   4. West (U.S.)—Intellectual life—
20th century.   5. Poetry—Authorship.   I. Title.

PS3563.A7879T88   2011
811'.509—dc22                                                          2010040236

*This Book Is for Three Amigos:*
*Dana Gioia, R. S. Gwynn and Michael Peich*

# Preface

When I wrote the title essay of this book my wife and I were living at 8,500 feet altitude in the Colorado Rockies, and though we have now moved more than 2,000 feet lower and are breathing more densely oxygenated air, I still feel an atmosphere of difference concerning poetry in the American West. Although my former town has grown, adding a Wal-Mart among other developments, and the Pikes Peak region now has its own poet laureate, poetry has a hard time being heard, and Western poets still feel the problem of distance within and between their communities. My decade in thinner air was exalting in some ways, yet there was a double-consciousness where the arts were concerned, a love-hate relationship governed in part by having the sublime in the form of vertiginous mountain views more or less up the street and the nearest art museum twenty miles away.

Other things have changed. I now live in a city, often getting about on a bike and seeing views that are less sublime. My verse novel about Colorado, *Ludlow,* has done much to solidify my own literary and cultural awareness of this place, and I have now written an opera libretto based upon *The Scarlet Letter* for composer Lori Laitman, who lives near Washington, D.C. Our oratorio, *Vedem,* premiered in Seattle, and we are working on a *Ludlow* opera. As a result, my sense of the isolation of the Western poet is not so intense as it used to be. The Internet revolution has changed everything about the life of the poet, including the culture of publication. There is no telling where it will take us, though I can't help thinking the fundamental culture of the poem—its values of orality and verbal precision—will not be much altered by these technological changes.

The essays in this book arise from years of wrestling with such things—the distances between us, nature versus art, art in nature and nature in art. People like me, born in the American West before overcrowding and the encroachment of a more conservative ethos, have surely had a different relationship to the arts than, say, a person raised in Manhattan or Philadelphia, where one assumes a rich cultural life will always be near at hand. I love the arts to distraction, but I also understand their absence, for better or worse—the apprehension of a world ungoverned by humanity and its creative impulses.

Essays in this book were written for a variety of purposes over several years. Sometimes they began as book reviews. "Some Narrative Poets of the American West" was a keynote address to the wonderful scholars of the Robinson Jeffers Association. The pieces on Grace Schulman and B. H. Fairchild were lectures given on the occasion of the Aiken-Taylor Award ceremonies at the University of the South. But nearly all of these essays concern notions of American poetry and poets—until the last two pieces, which take up the "West" in a broader fashion by musing on postcolonial studies and a Greek poet I happen to love, George Seferis. The center of the book contains three essays in praise of Anthony Hecht and Richard Wilbur, friends and mentors to whom I owe more than I can possibly repay.

Periodicals in which these pieces first appeared, often in different form, include the *Connecticut Review, Divide,* the *Hudson Review,* the *Sewanee Review,* the *Weekly Standard* and the *Writer's Chronicle.* Thanks are due to their editors for support and encouragement over the years. In addition, the piece called "Opening a Town" was commissioned by W. C. Jameson for a book that subsequently never appeared. "'The Contemplation of Horror Is Not Edifying': Anthony Hecht as a War Poet" was commissioned by Ernest Hilbert for a volume devoted to the poetry of my late friend and teacher. Fellow poets Annie Finch and Marilyn Hacker selected this book for publication, and Ellen Bauerle, Alexa Ducsay, and Marcia LaBrenz have been its able shepherds at the University of Michigan Press. I consider this a book of friendships as much as literary criticism—notes from the life of a reader. It is dedicated to three friends who have sustained me, fed me, amused me and taught me more than I can say.

# Acknowledgments

Most quotations in this book fall under fair use provisions, but where extended excerpts and whole poems have been quoted, permission has been sought. The author wishes to thank the following for permission to quote:

Michael Donaghy, "Machines" and "Local 32B" from *Collected Poems,* published by Picador, an imprint of Pan Macmillan. Copyright 2009 by the Estate of Michael Donaghy. Used by permission.

Suzanne J. Doyle, "Heart's Desire." Copyright 1992 by Suzanne J. Doyle. Reprinted by permission of the author.

B. H. Fairchild, "Angels" from *The Arrival of the Future,* Alice James Books, 2000. Used by permission of the publisher. Lines from *Early Occult Memory Systems of the Lower Midwest* copyright 2003 by B. H. Fairchild, used by permission of W. W. Norton & Company, Inc.

Anthony Hecht, "Once Removed," first published in *The Kenyon Review* Spring 1947, copyright 2011 by The Estate of Anthony Hecht. Used by permission of the Estate of Anthony Hecht. Lines from *Anthony Hecht in Conversation with Philip Hoy,* Between the Lines (an imprint of The Waywiser Press), 3rd edition, 2004. Used by permission of the publisher.

Thomas McGrath, "The Buffalo Coat," from *The Movie at the End of the World* by Thomas McGrath. Reprinted by permission of Ohio University Press/Swallow Press, Athens, Ohio (www .ohioswallow.com). Lines from *Letter to an Imaginary Friend* by

# Contents

# Two Minds of a Western Poet

Where I live        distance is the primal fact
—James Galvin

From my study window I look out on a stand of aspen trees mixed with a few spruce and pines, across the road more woods and the half-disguised houses of neighbors, each tactfully set on its half acre. A generation ago this was a dude ranch outside the mountain town of Woodland Park, Colorado. Relatives of mine worked here in those days—tourist wranglers. Now Paradise Estates is a bedroom community incorporated into the growing town, squeezed between Highway 24 and the national forest. Most of us commute twenty miles to Colorado Springs to make our livings.

Woodland Park is a town one drives through on the way to Cripple Creek or the Collegiate Range and beyond. From the highway it hardly resembles a community at all, just a line of nondescript shops and gas stations anchored by two supermarkets. You would have to turn off the highway to see a set of schools and a lot of churches, the old log cabins of what once was a summer town. Recently, local artists have been trying to convince city leaders that we need art. Art helps build communities, they argue, pointing to good evidence from other parts of the nation. Not wanting to seem philistine and wanting even less to pass up any economic opportunity, our leaders have sprinkled statuary here and there. Even the most powerful land developer in town sees dollar signs in his neighbors' goodwill efforts. Everyone tries to ignore the highway plowing through town with its increasing volume of traffic splitting the community in two.

This is the American West, or part of it, and I am a product of the West. I grew up in Bellingham, Washington, the middle son of two highly educated Coloradoans who had moved there after World War II. A recent newspaper story about the snipers in the Washington, D.C., area tells me the gunmen used to live in Bellingham, "a Mecca for people who want to be as far away as possible from wherever they are from." That's my hometown, which was a lot smaller when I lived there than it is now. It occurs to me that I must have been twenty years old before I saw great art in a museum. I certainly saw art in books and my parents' slides from a trip to Europe. There were works of local artists in our house, and I might have glimpsed others in museums in Seattle and Vancouver, B.C. A great poet, Theodore Roethke, lived in Seattle, and I had a book about the paintings of Mark Tobey. I got to know a bit of music because my high school girlfriend played the violin, my father listened to public radio, my older brother recorded albums on reel-to-reel tapes. Good theater existed in Seattle and at the Oregon Shakespeare Festival. I dozed through some opera, acted in high school plays.

At nineteen I unloaded crab and shrimp boats in Alaska for seven months—turning twenty in the Aleutians—then headed overseas, where I hitchhiked the perimeter of the British Isles and dallied on the Continent. I saw London's museums and bought Upper Circle tickets to every play on boards. I also saw plays in Edinburgh and Dublin. In the reading room of the British Museum I stared at original manuscripts of Yeats and Shaw, feeling embarrassed for the American girl cracking her chewing gum over the glass cases and exclaiming, "Jesus! Wow!" In Paris and Madrid I saw more great museums. I carried books in my rucksack and mailed them home when I had read them. I took in culture as I took in English beer—in huge swallows. I made sketches, notes, thought of myself as an artist, a real down-and-outer.

But drawn as I was to these famous centers of the arts, I was also happy to be hoofing it alone, all conversations internal or made with any kindly stranger who gave me a lift. Even the attractions of a city like Madrid could not hold me for long. I felt compelled to the margins and spent a month in Almería on the Costa Blanca, falling into a regular life of reading in cafes, swimming, exploring, flirting with Spanish girls, then returning to my pension to read some more and bother the neighbors with late-night hammering on my portable typewriter.

What we often call a cultural life, including all the boozy rebellion of the arts, was something I could only take in small doses. The greatest museums in the world made me feel claustrophobic after a while, and I hated competing with crowds even to see a masterpiece. I was a Westerner—an American far-Westerner, that is—from a small town, not a barrio, and crowds were alien to me. One moment I could enjoy their anonymity, the next I was fighting for air. In a forest I felt at home but starved for the sort of intensity art promises. In museums I felt alien, my culture-thirst slaked, my soul pummeled and quaking. I was born divided—perhaps not so uncommon a fate. Poetry is for me an attempt to find unity of being, and as such it is a meditative process made public through stories and forms.

As a product of the American West in the fifties and sixties, I am of two minds about that "cultural life." I desire the arts like some unpossessable diamond, yet I desire their absence with equal force. Without art I feel sick, half alive, yet cruising an empty highway or hiking under a glacier can sooth me like a prayer. After twenty years away from the West (living in Greece, New York, Pittsburgh and Minnesota) I'm happy to be back in a state where I have some roots and know the lay of the land. But Colorado is, like most states in the West, such a cultural backwater that I'm often driven to despair. One can live a lifetime here convinced that all the important values are Christian and commercial, using the Rockies only as a place to burn fuel and make noise. One can be completely unaware of Bierstadt's paintings of these landscapes, or even the peak that bears his name, let alone poets from Longfellow on down who have celebrated parts of the state. As a state of mind, Colorado is generally blank or cluttered with the sprawling dreck of contemporary America. Yet I am more at home here than in most places I have lived as an adult, and fully aware that landscapes like the one outside my window have shaped my writing as much as the wall of books beside my desk.

The two minds I refer to are not unrelated to the most ancient theories of art. Plato saw poets as vessels for sacred inspiration, making them dangerous to the ideal state. Some modern writers believe creativity comes straight from the uninhibited soul and requires no education or training. Traces of America's native Platonism can be found in poets from the Transcendentalists to the Beats. Aristotle, on the other hand, was the classifier of forms, suggesting that indeed some training in traditions was required of poets, and such notions can be traced forward to Longinus, Lu Chi, T. S. Eliot, etc. Most theories of poetry choose from a menu of ideas about inspiration or craft as if the twain could never meet, when in fact they *must* meet in the creation of good poems. Writing is in part an attempt to reconcile these warring factions within.

For most of us, America is like a wind blowing our voices away in the midst of each day's effort to speak. Yet I can't help feeling we have it worse in the West—something to do with the distances between us. Perhaps we are more attuned to change and blank indifference, creatures of sprawl and space, our geological consciousness almost impervious to graffiti or poems.

&

> . . . I died without nails, without a copy of the
> *Atlantic Monthly*. . . .
> —Charles Bukowski

The West is made of watersheds. The Missouri River, fed by the Yellowstone, the Bighorn, the Powder, the Platte, flows into the Mississippi drainage to be joined by the Arkansas. Northwest, the Snake, the Columbia, the Willamette, and moving south, the Russian, the Sacramento, the San Joaquin—these find the Pacific at various points on the coast. Then you have the major drainages of the Rio Grande and the Colorado, without which life in the Southwest would be inconceivable.

Use the Missouri as a line drawn east and south, then at Kansas City pick up the eastern borders of Kansas, Oklahoma and Texas; you've got a pretty good place to start defining the West as a region, taking into account its components: the Plains, the Rockies, the Southwest, Northwest, California and Texas. Rivers and mountains are the veins and bones of this sprawled body. Gary Snyder chose well when he titled his long poem

*Mountains and Rivers without End.* And Louis Simpson had the right idea in his poem "The Redwoods," which begins,

> Mountains are moving, rivers
> are hurrying. But we
> are still.
>
> We have the thoughts of giants—
> clouds, and at night the stars.

Simpson's move from landscape to mind reminds me that geography helps, but not enough. There is a West of the mind. There is a West of many minds. The enclaves of religious fundamentalists, the back road survivalists, the developers, the greens, the tramps, the ski bums and bookworms and barrio gangs, the vast neighborhoods of the newly arrived, the computer geeks and ex-dot-commers. The West is like an imaginary marketplace where visions rise and fall. One invests in pasts as well as futures.

I had read Simpson's poem before, but had not been struck by it as I was when I opened *Poems of the American West* (Everyman Editions, 2002), an anthology edited by Robert Mezey, and stumbled on it again. "O if there is a poet," Simpson writes, "let him come now!" He's arrived at the terminus of American expansion, the end of the Open Road, but finds something as yet unexpressed in the land itself. I know what he means. Born at the tail end of 1954, I grew up with a strong sense that it had all been seen and done, we had reached our limits, but I was troubled by an equally strong conviction that much remained to be said.

Mezey's anthology is a good place to start, not least because of his humility before so vast a subject. "I am as little qualified as most poets or scholars," he writes in his foreword, "to set up as an authority on the poetry of the American West. True, I grew up in West Philadelphia, and have spent most of the last thirty-five years in the West, mostly in California, but neither accident has given me the slightest confidence that I know what the West is, or even where it is." An accomplished poet and translator, Mezey has also been one of our most intriguing anthologists, from the *Naked Poetry* volumes of the sixties and seventies, edited with Stephen Berg, to his superb Modern Library edition of *The Poetry of Edwin Arlington Robinson* (1999). His taste is catholic in the best sense—like his friend Donald Justice he has written marvelous poems in both free verse and meter—and is reflected in the poems chosen for the new book.

Most anthologists these days collect *poets* for the purpose of building careers. But in this case Mezey collects *poems,* and therein lies a lesson. He is not necessarily interested in promoting writers who live in the West, however one defines the region. I appreciate the personal touch in Mezey's selection, the willed eccentricity of a book called *Poems of the American West* that includes work by Guillaume Apollinaire, Zbigniew Herbert and Rhina Espaillat. Mezey acknowledges that West of the mind I mentioned earlier, finds aspects of its mythos in poems from all over the world.

Taking this strategy to heart, one could make a very fat anthology. Cowboys and Western landscapes show up in some surprising places. Off the cuff I think of Seamus Heaney defining Ireland as a place without prairies, and one could no doubt find poets from Asian countries making use of the American West as a source of irony or dream of freedom. As Mezey himself admits, his book is not definitive, nor could it be. It is instead an eclectic compendium mostly of good poems arising from physical experiences of place as well as from mental geographies. He includes a selection of traditional Native American poems in translation as well as a fair representation of living poets of various backgrounds, and he does not exclude Country and Western lyrics or traditional songs like John Phillips's mordant "Me and My Uncle" and Fred Koller's "Lone Star State of Mind":

> And here I sit alone in Denver,
> Sippin' the California wine,
> And I've got all night to remember you—
> I'm in a Lone Star state of mind.

Mezey reminds us that Robert Frost spent his early years as an urban Californian. It irked me that he included Frost's misguided poem "The Gift Outright" until I saw it echoed nearly two hundred pages later in Larry Levis's "The Poet at Seventeen." Far from endorsing Manifest Destiny, Mezey merely points out how powerful a myth it remains. I am also glad to see strong work by Charles Bukowski, James Galvin, B. H. Fairchild, Mark Jarman, Timothy Murphy, Ted Kooser, Nancy Ware and others. There are poems by the brilliant student of Donald Justice, Joe Bolton, who committed suicide and whose work Justice generously edited. And there is a knockout of a poem by Suzanne Doyle, "Heart's Desire":

> Somewhere above King's Canyon, having crossed
> An unmarked pass, tonight you'll make your bed
> In alpine air, lay down your tender head
> Among the rocks that glaciers ground and tossed
> Within that wide angle of time: the Ice Age.
> This is the country of your heart's desire,
> The granite cut to peaks, luring you higher,
> The mind but blood and muscle schooled for passage.
> You stare into the stellar void and wait.
> Empty, alone, the god can enter in
> Not so unlike the fiend who was your fate,
> The one that took you small, again, again,
> Broke you in two and still might break you more.
> It is inhuman beauty, cold, austere,
> You open to receive without a fear,
> Arousing your remote and shattered core
> To the release that only it can bring:
> Annihilation of the self by Nothing.

I ponder that last line with its nearly Buddhist promise and wonder if the annihilation of the self by Nothing isn't also a condition of the American West, a blessed curse of living where I do. But just as I grasp it the image blurs and evaporates like breath on a windowpane.

King's Canyon, the setting of Doyle's poem, was also a favorite setting for Kenneth Rexroth, who can be found in these pages with J. V. Cunningham, Yvor Winters, Gary Snyder, John Haines, William Stafford, Edgar Bowers, Timothy Steele, R. S. Gwynn, Alberto Rios, Ron Koertge, Lawson Fusao Inada, Suzanne Lummis, Olivia Simpson Ellis and N. Scott Momaday.

Mezey has cast a wide net but pursed it tightly, printing no poem that he did not genuinely like. The fact that his taste will not always be yours or mine does not really matter. One reads anthologies like this one partly to escape one's preconceptions.

Still, the book lacks two poems I wish it had included, by Thomas McGrath and Richard Wilbur. McGrath was such an uneven writer that one has to look hard for his best work. Born in North Dakota, he was known for his communist sympathies, which in his bad work bent him toward propaganda. But he was also a spirited writer about the West, as you can see in his short lyric "The Buffalo Coat":

> I see him moving, in his legendary fleece,
> Between the superhighway and an Algonquin stone axe;
> Between the wild tribes, in their lost heat,
> And the dark blizzard of my Grandfather's coat;
> Cold with the outdoor cold caught in the curls,
> Smelling of the world before the poll tax.
>
> And between the new macadam and the Scalp Act
> They got him by the short hair; had him clipped
> Who once was wild—and all five senses wild—
> Printing the wild with his hoof's inflated script
> Before the times was money in the bank,
> Before it was a crime to be so mild.
>
> But history is a fact, and moves on feet
> Sharper than his, toward wallows deeper than.
> And the myth that covered all his moving parts,
> Grandfather's time had turned into a coat;
> And what kept warm then, in the true world's cold
> Is old and cold in a world his death began.

That "world his death began" is, in a sense, the West I inhabit as I write this, my house perched on a hill between the South Platte and the Arkansas, on the north shoulder of Pikes Peak, a mountain that inspired both "America the Beautiful" and a moronic road race.

The second poem I miss in Mezey's anthology, Richard Wilbur's "Piccola Commedia," recalls a year in which the young poet tramped across America prior to his service in World War

II. The poem is too long to quote here, but I would add it to Mezey's anthology because of its vivid evocation of fallen dreams and the transience I associate with the West. I find it again in J. V. Cunningham's poems. And Donald Justice writing of Henry James in California: "The sad-faced monsters of the plains are gone; / Wall Street controls the wilderness."

Where is the American West? My definitions scatter. It's in the helicopter cowboys over Saigon. It's in *The Sands of Iwo Jima* with—who else?—John Wayne. It's in the Japanese grocer huddled against Seattle rain, the *campesinos* playing one-armed bandits on a reservation in California. The old Monument Valley of John Ford has its mythology, and while that mythology will not suffice it also will not die away. Maybe the American West is in those snipers who left my hometown and crossed the country on a trail of bodies. The stories are too many to be told, which means the poets still have much to tell us.

&

> Transience is not symbolic, it is real
> In the unfurnished places of our lives
> So bare of ghosts. . . .
> —Charles Gullans

Before me a window full of trees; to my left a wall of books. The latter includes a six-volume edition of the complete works of Charles Dickens, large illustrated tomes with double columns of small print. They were published in New York by P. F. Collier, and though they bear no copyright date they must be from the late nineteenth century. Each volume is signed inside:

> Geo. Mason
> Shelbina
> Mo.

This would be my great-grandfather George. His father, Abraham, had come west from Kentucky and edited a newspaper in Paris, Missouri. Each generation lugged what bits of cultural life it could carry on the journey west. But they wouldn't have chosen such an arduous path if they hadn't been restless, eager for new life. It was George who made his way to Colorado, eventually running a mercantile store in Cedar Hill for coal miners. South of Pueblo and north of Trinidad, Cedar Hill was more a camp than a town, a few shacks and a lot of tents, I suppose. Such vanished towns are an image of the West for me. There have been other deserted villages in other countries, but I know of no landscape quite so marked by transience as the American West.

A more famous camp than Cedar Hill was at Ludlow. When miners in those communities went on strike, John D. Rockefeller's henchmen used their influence to send in troops, a measure culminating in the Ludlow Massacre of April 1914. By then, after acting as postmaster in the town of Walsenburg, George Mason had moved to Trinidad, a town on the Purgatory River, just north of the New Mexican border. Bat Masterson was once sheriff of Trinidad, and the famous train robber Black Jack was hanged on one of the town's streets. George went partners in a creamery, and soon manufactured Mason's Ice Cream with 20 percent butterfat instead of the minimum requirement of 10 percent. Their advertisements proclaimed, "MASON'S ICE CREAM—BETTER THAN THE LAW REQUIRES!"

I have a photograph of George and his four brothers as young men, taken in St. Louis, and they look like a reunion of the James Gang. I knew George's son Abraham, my grandfather, as well as several of Abe's siblings. They were all characters. Abe ran off to Idaho as a young man, then crossed into Canada and joined the Seaforth Highlanders. He wore a kilt and fought with the regiment in World War I. At the Battle of Amiens he was carrying ammunition cases for a machine gun when a bullet or shell fragment went through his hand. The ammunition cases stopped that lead from piercing his chest and killing him. After the war Abe returned to Trinidad with Ethel, the sweetheart he'd met in the Northwest, and they raised four red-headed boys, the eldest of whom was my father.

Abe could be a hell-raiser when he wanted. My uncle Frank remembered him coming home drunk, explaining he had stopped off at so-and-so's to say hello, and Ethel would help him into bed saying, "Oh, Abe, look what you done to yourself."

But the man I remember was a calm, good-natured fellow

who looked a lot like the actor Wallace Beery, smoked unfiltered cigarettes and took my brothers and me on long walks in the mesa country where we searched for arrowheads. My father had started him on that hobby back in the Dustbowl days when topsoil blew to hell and gone and ancient artifacts lay exposed for the picking. I grew up with old flint points, stone axes, *metates*, bone necklaces and even a rawhide medicine bag my father had traded for.

It was Abe who helped turn the creamery into a candy manufacturing company, so most males in my family were drummers selling TOMA, the Mason brand, in Colorado, New Mexico and the Western plains. My uncle Frank was a drummer for years, then took over the company when Abe retired. The price of sugar rose in the early seventies, driving them out of business, and eventually Frank left Trinidad for work outside Denver.

My father was the son who got as far away as he could. He used to save his paper route money, hitchhike up to Colorado Springs or down to Raton and take flying lessons in biplanes—this in 1936, when he was fifteen. Though he could hardly swim, he got himself selected for the Naval Academy when war broke out. His class was rammed through Annapolis in three years, fresh fodder for the Pacific War. Three of the four Mason brothers served in World War II, and once they came home on leave at the same time and a photograph of them with their freckles removed was splashed on front pages across the country. The old photographer who removed their freckles used to make his living taking pictures of dead people and Indians.

My father married a Colorado girl, Evelyn Peterson, whose own father had once been a coal miner and had somehow become a doctor in Grand Junction. Evelyn's nickname was "Pete." Jim and Pete, my parents, eventually settled in Bellingham, "a Mecca for people who want to be as far away as possible from wherever they are from." For years I thought I had motion sickness—in this case an illness that means you will always be on the move.

Bellingham was a good place for my brothers and me to grow up. We had the run of the woods, lakes and mountains nearby. Despite all our troubles—my parents' eventual divorce, my mother's alcoholism, which she has fought bravely to overcome, my brother Doug's death while climbing Mt. Shuksan, the most beautiful peak in the North Cascades—we were not such a bad family. My parents worshipped education and encouraged any spark of ambition in their boys. But that desire to get out of town hit me hard at eighteen, and most of my adult life I have been on the move.

ॐ

Eyes like small veiled moons
circling our single light, sleek
shadows with pawprints,
all went with the outfit; and
youth, a river of campfires.
—Rhina Espaillat

I won't pretend to like what is happening to the West. I don't like unbridled and tasteless development of land or water wasted on lawns. I don't like endless chains of strip malls, insane traffic, self-righteous boosterism, the endless variety of machines making noise and eroding soil in the mountains.

Of course, I'm part of the problem, aren't I? I don't live downtown and get about on a bike. I live on my wooded plot, just below a hill where many new houses will eventually be built, and like my neighbors I commute, usually alone due to my busy life, burning up gas and polluting the air.

As boys my brothers and I were outdoors all the time—sailing, skiing, climbing, hiking, sleeping under the stars. More often we slept under the rain. We were expert at building shelters with plastic tarps and bits of rope. I can't tell you how many days and nights of my youth were spent huddled under wet plastic, waiting for rain to stop, firing up the Primus stove to make cocoa or soup. I walked glaciers and snowfields as a boy, saw seals dive from British Columbian rocks, played Tarzan in the woods, pretending the long stems of bracken ferns were poison spears. We had to entertain ourselves. Very few people in the world, especially in our time, ever grow up with the freedom I enjoyed as a child. It may be something Americans have lost forever.

I was also lucky in my parents' friends, who loved to read and talk about everything under the sun. I grew up listening to people who were interested in the world, who could read the wind on Bellingham Bay and used days off to take their families into the mountains. They were generally left of center in their politics, agnostics who raised us without religious turmoil. My father began as an Eisenhower Republican but by the time of Nixon declared he was a Socialist. Yet when he read of some random murder in Seattle he swung to a primal belief in revenge, saying that even hanging was too good for these killers. He joined Beyond War. He smoked pot. He took LSD with two friends up in the mountains, and wrote pages of notes about the trip. His favorite literary character was Joyce Cary's Gulley Jimson, a model of creative irresponsibility, but he stayed true to his sons and helped us any way he could. He was a character of the West, I think—impulsive, contradictory, driven to succeed and fighting that drive in himself.

My mother, on the other hand, was someone for whom just leading a normal life seemed nearly impossible. Like her own mother—the Scottish grandmother I never met—she was an addict. Her mother had become a nurse, eventually losing jobs when she was caught stealing drugs. She ended up lobotomized in St. Louis, a real skeleton in the closet. My mother was smart and beautiful and haunted by more demons than most people could stand. I gave her up for dead so often that I, too, was haunted. I was afraid if I stopped moving my ghosts would catch up to me.

But the woman who once was a cause of my own rootlessness has, late in life, fought free of addiction, found real friends in AA, worked at her friendships and her citizenship with genuine humility, bearing her grief and her guilt and finding that uncanny humor recovering addicts have, everything leveled and cleared for rebuilding. My mother has put down roots. She has become a pillar of her community, someone to emulate and honor for the very simplicity of her life. This is the greatest gift she could possibly have given her two surviving sons. Because of what she has done, each of us now looks at life with a new sense of possibility and hope. My younger brother has become a father. I'm a stepfather and grandfather. Maybe I will put down roots too. Lately I have tried in poems to root myself in this place, to affirm something of value in living here even with the problems I have been mentioning. This is the only way I know to make two minds into one.

For most of us in the West, culture in that vague and desirable sense I've been using is not given but acquired, and not easily acquired at that. I think of poets I know in Colorado: Anne Waldman at Naropa, Mary Crow at Fort Collins, Mark Irwin in Salida when he can get there, Jim Tipton raising bees and writing poems in Grand Junction, Rosemerry Trommer running a poetry circle in Telluride, the wild David Rothman in Crested Butte, where he used to run a prep school in an old motel, publishing books at Conundrum Press and pushing a music festival on a ski town, Mark Todd on a ranch near Gunnison, Laurie Wagner Buyer in Woodland Park when she isn't in Texas. I also think of Steven Wingate and others crazy enough to run literary magazines. We're all so far away from each other. It takes enormous effort, exhausting effort, to make a literary life in such a place. Most Colorado taxpayers would rather support missile defense systems than any of the arts. But there has always been a necessary stubbornness in the act of creation. Even the tug-of-war between art and wilderness in souls like mine has not been bad for poetry, to use that one example. Our challenge in the West is to recognize the facts of living where we do, learn the lay of the land and its place in the larger world, and try to hold our voices steady in the wind.

# Opening a Town

A gravel crossroads. Stand there at the X and place yourself, and maybe your *self* will vanish in the time folds of the land. You are someone else. You are no one. All being flickers like a lit match. To the west a scrawl of foothills, mine shafts, canyons, pine and scree slopes. To the east a forested rise known as the Black Hills. Face south and a town grows in all the smoke of industry: Ludlow, Colorado. It is April 20, 1914, one of the worst days in American labor history. There by the water tank, just beyond the saloon, the school, the railroad platform, National Guard troopers have set up their machine gun. An officer looks toward you, then beyond you, through binoculars.

Now look north to the flat land filled with tents. A little city of immigrants, twelve hundred of them speaking a Babel of tongues. The tents are burning, most of the people fled to a broad arroyo beyond your sight.

This is where Louis Tikas stood, but who was Louis Tikas? A union organizer caught up in the strike and subsequent battles, an immigrant like nearly everyone else in the camp. He had tried his hand at coal mining and knew the horrible conditions in the mines. Four months ago he had become an American citizen, learning the hard way how often this country is reborn in blood. He was a name acquired in far-off cities, a young man of Crete who knew a bit of English. In the dark and firelight the shooting and smoke and soldiers were the last things he would have seen. That night he and Jim Fyler and John Bartolotti would be taunted, beaten and shot, their bodies left beside the rail bed for three days, until it was safe enough to haul them twelve miles south to the town of Trinidad for public funerals.

That was the Ludlow Massacre, or some version of it. You have come back to stand here at the X and lose yourself. You are a pebble of coal, a strand of fence line, a magpie watching from a post. The hollowing wind picks up a fistful of dirt and tosses it across the road to where the bodies lay.

Apparently the three men ran. They were shot in the back.

Apparently they were trying to stop the fight that had raged all day, but someone wanted them dead. Someone wanted to clear the camp. Erase the immigrants. On April 20 more than a score of people were killed.

Stand at the X and wonder who they were, and you might as well be wondering who you are, what mark, if any, you will leave when the wind kicks up your dust.

¾

Now I recall a Mason family reunion west of Trinidad at Stonewall Gap. Picnics on the Purgatory River. A clan of joke-tellers, leg-pullers, yarn-swappers. And someone says we should try to find Cedar Hill, the town where George Mason, my great-grandfather, ran one of the notorious company stores. The stores took illegal scrip instead of cash, upped the prices, cheated the miners—one reason they had gone out on strike. But the business got George started in the West, got him his toehold after he came out from Missouri in the 1890s.

So we piled into cars and caravanned into the desert under the foothills of the Front Range, looking for Cedar Hill. We found concrete slabs that might have been foundations. We found a mine shaft squinting shut, a hard-plated piece of ground littered with bits of earthenware, a fragment of China doll in a faded dress.

Late summer sunlight glinted off the ground. Was this Cedar Hill? None of us knew. We stopped at the Ludlow monument where uncles told of the massacre, and I stood somewhere near the X not knowing it marked the spot where Louis Tikas died.

One of my great-uncles was born at Tabasco, back in a nearby canyon. His older brother, Abe, was my grandfather. By this time Abe lay in the Masonic Cemetery in Trinidad, not far from the grave of Tikas. But the story of Louis Tikas was still largely untold, waiting for Zeese Papanikolas to write his book, *Buried Unsung: Louis Tikas and the Ludlow Massacre*.

Like so many Americans we stood there gawking at a landscape without knowing its story. We did not know how bound we were to this dry, unforgiving land. It felt exotic to us, a film set without a script, a director or a crew to bring it to life.

We never did find Cedar Hill.

ᶻ᷄

In 2007 I published a book called *Ludlow,* a verse novel, which is a strange animal. Somehow the verse did not scare away readers. The book struck a nerve. I gave dozens of readings from it all over the United States, but the Colorado readings had a special *frisson.* When I read in Trinidad, a man admonished me for praising Zeese Papanikolas's version of events. "That book made me furious," he said. "It was so biased I threw it across the room."

Nerves are still sensitive concerning Ludlow. Some families are tied to the company, some to the strikers. The politics are raw, the scores unsettled.

I read in Denver with Scott Martelle and Eleanor Swanson, who had also published books about Ludlow. Afterward a dignified gentleman with a gray beard came up to me and said, "I am going to buy your book. But I don't like what you said about my grandfather." He was a descendent of Billy Reno, mentioned only briefly as "the company's chief thug" in my opening chapter. I was learning about the uses of history in a work of fiction.

When I read in Montrose, Colorado, I met Dan Beshoar, whose father, Barron, had known my own father in Trinidad. Dan's grandfather and great-grandfather were doctors who sided with the strikers against the company. As a boy Dan had known John Lawson, the Scottish immigrant who organized the southern Colorado coal strike in 1913 and whose career as a union man was terminated by the Ludlow Massacre. Opinions differ about Lawson, but I admire him. After the massacre, he was hung out to dry by union higher-ups, reduced to working in the mines again with a pick and shovel, until his hard work was observed and he rose with stunning irony to a management position. Still, the miners remembered Ludlow. They remembered all Lawson had done for the cause. If Lawson makes the contract, they said, we will sign it.

Dan Beshoar has sent me some photographs. Among them I find Lawson with Mother Jones and Horace Hawkins, Lawson with Louis Tikas and one Robert Harlan, later mayor of Seattle. There is a photo of the "death pit" at Ludlow where thirteen women and children suffocated when flames overtook the tents. In another photo Frank Rubino lies on a slab, a victim of the shooting that day. Then there is the funeral of the children held in Trinidad at the Catholic church, not far from another church in which my own parents would be married following World War II. In photos of the Ludlow camp after the fires you can see scraps of metal stoves and bed frames, all that survived the flames. It is a bitter thing to look upon, no matter what your politics.

Finally there is a photo of John Lawson as an old man, standing in front of the Ludlow monument. A big man in a suit and spectacles, still fit as a boxer but with an aura of intellect about him.

"You knew John Lawson?" I asked Dan Beshoar. "What was his voice like?"

"Deep. Gravelly. Rough."

As a child Dan had sat on the old man's lap and listened to his stories. It was a baptism, of sorts, a ritual acknowledgment of suffering and rage.

Emotions about Ludlow run deep in families, in what children grown to adulthood can remember of their own flesh and blood.

❧

Heading south on Interstate 25, you could miss Ludlow if you blinked. Not much is left of the old mining towns of that violent time. This is southeastern Colorado, where the mountains drop down to dry mesa country. You've gone south of the exit for Walsenburg, south of another for Aguilar, and you're maybe a dozen miles north of Trinidad, a far more significant town than many Americans, or even Coloradoans, realize. If you're on the freeway here you're usually headed to Albuquerque or points beyond. You're not thinking that pivotal moments in American history happened here, that Mother Jones was dodging the law to get into Trinidad and dramatize the plight of the miners, that John D. Rockefeller Jr., who owned a controlling interest in the Colorado Fuel and Iron Company, had hired Eastern executives to run his operations in the coal fields here and the executives hired detectives to enforce their rules, that Governor Ammons, a Democrat who came to office on the coattails of Woodrow Wilson, would panic at the shootouts between strikers and company goons and call in the National Guard, that the Guard would side with the company against the strikers, that President Wilson himself would be watching bulletins from the fight and after the massacre would put federal troops in place to stop the killing.

No, you're usually just on the freeway, which means you're not seeing much of anything. You're anxious to get someplace. You might be thinking the real Colorado is the I-70 corridor, which takes skiers west from Denver to places like Vail and Aspen.

Many Coloradoans are new to the state and don't really know where they are. They don't know the names of the buttes and rivers. I wanted to find words for this landscape:

A solitary cone of rock rose up
from lacerated land, the dry arroyos,
scars that scuppered water in flood season
down to a river. In dusty summertime
the cottonwoods eked out a living there
in a ragged line below the high peaks.
The ground was a plate of stony scutes that shone
like diamonds at noon, an hour when diamondbacks

coiled on sunbaked rocks. Or so I pictured
in color films imagination shot.
The butte they called *El Huerfano,* alone
east of the highway . . . We were driving south,
and to the west the heat-waved mountains rose,
abrasive peaks without a trace of snow,
bare rocks above a belt of evergreens.
This was my father's home. My father had

a childhood here, so far away from mine,
and knew of mines in the long-vanished towns,
a butte the Mexicans had named "the Orphan,"
and two peaks Indians called the *Huajatollas,*
"Breasts of the Earth." . . .

Sailors know scuppers are the drains in bilges of a boat. Scutes are like the armored plates on an armadillo's back. I wanted the "sc" sound of both words for its harshness, an aural version of the scattered sun-glint off the land itself.

It does not matter to me if readers fail to notice such effects in *Ludlow*. Some readers will read for the story, others for the words, still others for the interplay of the two. I'm a writer. I'll take any readers I can get.

                                        ❧

Poets taking up historical subjects face many problems. One of these is the patina of documentary fact, which can flatten the imaginative texture of the writing. Too much political poetry attempts to accrue virtue by virtue of its subject, as if righteousness alone were sufficient for art.

I wanted to avoid that. I wanted the roughness, obscenity and vitality of life pulsing in my lines. The immigrants who went on strike in 1913 were not angels. They were human beings. Scott Martelle has determined that in roughly nine months of skirmishes the strikers probably killed more people than the troops and company goons did—not that plenty of blood wasn't spilled on both sides.

I wanted vitality, not virtue.

Fiction proved a way into the story, a way to ground it in the reality of flesh, not fact. That was why I invented Luisa Mole and started years before the massacre. Her orphanhood—the immigrants nickname her *la Huerfana* after the butte I described earlier—is an existential problem more than a political one. It ties her to me, in a way, through a distant memory of childhood vulnerability. So I followed the lead of writers like Milan Kundera and introduced myself into the story, admitted my own motives as well as those of my characters.

Critics have noticed Luisa's name resembles that of Louis Tikas, also a character in my book, but have wondered why I paired the names when the two characters never really meet. Perhaps the two are paired through a third—myself, the narrator who occasionally appears, trying to piece the story together. The book arose from my sympathy for and identification with both figures. I used epigraphs in Spanish and Greek as deliberate clues that the book is about more than politics. I am standing at the gravel X, trying to know the reality of the self in this landscape, and I see this as the dilemma of many Americans. We move through the world as if our location were unimportant, feeling only marginally connected to what we see around us. Perhaps my identification with Louis and Luisa, one part fiction, the other wholly so, is an effort to understand my own complicated being. I am the X connecting these two troubled characters.

Of course my characters have more pressing problems than this—survival itself, for example—but they too live on multiple levels. They dream, they aspire. Their dreams and aspirations are lost in that fistful of dust blown across the road.

≥∙

It would not do to have a photograph on the cover of the book, because photographs tend toward the documentary. The book is grounded in dream and imagination. The painting chosen for the cover of *Ludlow* actually depicts a California landscape. My friend Mark Jarman recognized this at once and could tell me approximately what view was represented there. That is fine with me. Call it an image of aspiration, an ideal unmet at the crossroads where Louis died.

One chapter of the book, "The Photo in the Photo," describes an image that actually exists in the Colorado Historical Society collection. Taken by Oliver Aultman, a Trinidad photographer, this image of a dark-haired girl is pinned to an easel and re-photographed, a perfect example of postmodern remove, rather like what I attempt in the book's narrative voice. But even that photo-within-a-photo would appear too documentary in style, anchoring my story in history rather than in the literary truth of imagination, so I set it aside in favor of the painting.

It is vitality I am after, not virtue. Presence, not truth in an objective sense. The problem of knowing will not be solved when the story has been told, yet I hope that a *felt* approximation will occur, something like a remembered dream.

≥∙

If I write in any way for myself, as the cliché would have it, I write for the feeling of presence, awareness. I want to locate myself in the world, but just as certainly I vanish in that dust kicked up across the road. I do not know why the sense of my own reality has always been so tenuous, why other people have been more real to me than I am to myself, but this minor neurosis is certainly bound up in the how and why of writing. Here is a personal passage from late in the book:

> Windblown aridity in early spring,
> piñon, prickly pear, the struggling scrub.
> At noon my shadow pooled beneath my boots,
> my eyes surveying ground a step ahead
> for arrowheads or any signs of life,
> out walking a friend's ranch with Abraham,
> the land a maze of dry arroyos, slabs
> of pale rock, the flints exposed by weather.
>
> There too the terrible remains of winter,
> dead cattle caught in a raging blizzard
> lay unthawed in postures of resignation.
> I was so intent on treasure that I stumbled
> into a ditch and fell across the corpse
> of a calf the wild coyotes dined upon,
> a gutted leathery thing—it had a face
> and I started backwards, stifling a scream.
>
> What was I? Twelve years old? The age I dreamed
> Luisa Mole out foraging for water . . .
> On our visits south
> I begged to be taken out to the mesa country
> as if those afternoons on skeletal land
> put me in touch with some essential code,
> the remnants of a people who moved through,
> migrating hunters five millennia past.
>
> Look for a bench, land flat enough to camp on,
> a nearby source of water—there you'd find
> the silicates in flakes, clear fracture marks
> where fletchers made their tools, the midden washed
> by wind and flash floods all across the scarp.
> Nothing remained in place here. Even trees
> had shallow roots. In dustbowl days my father
> picked up points by the dozen on this land,

pot-hunting like his neighbors, half in love
with science, more with the electric touch
of hands across receded seas of time.
What had we found? I knew this evidence
of other lives had meaning of some sort.
I saw the strangers, grew among them for years
in my own mind. But was it love or envy?
Was it only pride of place? A kind of theft?

Always looking at the ground beneath my boots,
always listening for the call of Abraham
who'd find a point and let me think I found it,
whose meaty, sun-burnt hands would leave the pool
of wide-brimmed shade, point beyond scarred boots
to the perfect knife, worked like a stone leaf
and left there by the ancient wanderers,
original, aboriginal, and magic.

*Ludlow* is a book of evidence, not a concluded case. The only
verdict is loss.

Still, a poet has to laugh sometimes at his own pretenses. I
have begun a correspondence with Doug Minnis, a retired professor who grew up in Trinidad and knew my grandfather well.
Doug pointed out he never heard my grandfather referred to as
Abraham, only as Abe. I had to go for the biblical resonance,
didn't I? Books mythologize as much as they tell the truth.

ॐ

My father was the small-town boy who got away. War provided
him an exit from Trinidad—the Naval Academy, then Iwo Jima,
where his ship was hit by enemy fire. He survived, married, went
to medical school, moved to Bellingham, Washington, where I
was born and raised. But Trinidad was never far from us in family lore with its dry mesas and Purgatory River. I loved going
there. I loved seeing Abe and Ethel, my loquacious grandmother, my uncle Frank and his four children.

Frank could tell a story like nobody else. He told me about
the old dance hall in town with a floor on giant springs to absorb the traffic of shuffling feet—the very floor where Louis
Tikas may have danced with Pearl Jolly, a married woman with
whom he is rumored to have had an affair. As a boy Frank rode

rodeo until a bull threw him in the dirt. "Peeled off the whole front of my face," Frank said with a cigarette laugh. "Boy, I walked around for weeks and the whole front of my face was one big scab." It's cowboy hyperbole. To Frank we were equals in the kingdom of laughter. "That old boy," he said of someone else, "he looked like he'd been drug through a knothole."

Frank liked to fix things. In the war he fixed airplane engines on a Pacific island. He came home in his sailor suit, married Margie, and went to work for Abe at the candy company. On hot summer days he rolled a pack of cigarettes up, sailor-fashion, in the short sleeve of his T-shirt.

The Mason Candy Company had a brand name, TOMA, and a logo depicting an adobe pueblo. It made hard candy and chocolate mints and a few specialty items, selling them in south-eastern Colorado and the bordering states. Frank worked as a drummer at first, and years later he told how he opened up a town. He drove into some dusty place in Kansas or Oklahoma, cruised up and down the streets to check out the competition. Then he booked himself a motel room, sat on the edge of the bed with the phone book on his lap and started cold-calling stores that might sell candy, making good use of his gift for the gab.

Writing a book like *Ludlow* is a bit like opening up a town, try-ing to make contact with a place, find out who lives there, charm them into buying what you've got to sell. I have always thought writing should be tied to the way people talk. The fur-ther writing moves from actual speech, the more removed it is from vitality. Often the voice I heard in my head was Frank's, often my father's, sometimes Abe's.

Late on a Saturday night in Trinidad Frank and Marge came home from some motel where she had played bass and he drums in a jazz combo, and they had danced when others sat in, and smoked their voices raw. I remember loving it when they came home and laughter filled the house on Victoria Square and nobody cared the kids were still awake. My own parents were moving toward divorce and a shell of alienation covered each of us, but in Frank's house there always seemed to be the coherence of family.

I'm standing at the X again. X marks the spot. Dust devils cross the road.

When Abe died Frank took over the company, but he ran into bad luck. After Marge's sudden death and the failure of the business, Frank moved north of Denver. He remarried and lived in the trailer in Longmont. Not long after Alzheimer's killed my father, cancer and heart trouble got Frank. The other two brothers, Jack and Tom, are gone now as well. The four red-headed Mason boys of Trinidad, Colorado are dead.

The only verdict is loss.

❧

Writing *Ludlow* in verse, I knew I had precedents from Homer to the present day. Contemporary poets like Brad Leithauser, Glyn Maxwell and Les Murray had all written novels in verse. But *Ludlow* is not easy to define. It is not quite a novel, not quite an epic in the classical sense. Reviewers and readers have been kind to it, but my fellow poets do not always know what to make of it. Sometimes a book does not behave as we expect it to, and maybe it is all right that *Ludlow* perplexes some literati. It is a book I had to write when I had to write it. It is everything I knew at the time about Colorado, about stories and about poetry. So be it. After years of reading and thought I felt an accumulation of energy and knew it was a book. I read about Louis Tikas, born Ilias Spantidakis in Crete, and I knew something of his story because I have lived in Greece, speak reasonable Greek, and have many friends caught up in the double-consciousness of the immigrant, the way you dream in one language and wake to another.

When I invented a Scotsman named Too Tall MacIntosh who would join the strikers, I was in part remembering my own Scottish ancestry. But I was also recalling John Lennox, my beloved father-in-law, who had brought his wife and two daughters to America. When I wrote the book, John's widow, Hetty, was living under our roof, shyly regaling us with Ayrshire memories.

"Hetty, there's a full moon tonight. Tell us what you did back home on the night of a full moon."

"Oh, the full moon—that was when we went to visit the neighbors."

They needed a full moon to see their way home in the dark.

I laced the language of *Ludlow* with Scots, bits of Greek and Spanish, because I wanted a texture of words as wealthy as the stories of the place. I wanted, as far as my powers could manage it, an enrichment of American idioms, not from books but from talk.

The way John Lennox used to talk about Bobbie Burns— "That man had th' advantage o' the Scottish dialect as well as the English language"—guided me as much as my own reading of other dialect writers. Among those writers I would list Derek Walcott, so gifted with the macaronic language of his Caribbean island home. Whether my resolution succeeded or failed is out of my hands now.

ï¤

Abe and Ethel Mason lie a little ways to the north of Louis Tikas in the Masonic Cemetery of Trinidad. When I stand at Louis's grave, Fisher's Peak is off to the east, one of the most beautiful flat-topped mesas in the American West, with the sleepy town at its foot. Surrounding Louis's grave are head-stones inscribed in Japanese, Hungarian, Polish, Italian . . . This story is part of America's story. The local is national. The ordinary is extraordinary. American poets are constantly redis-covering such things.

Whatever my literary influences, whatever I have imitated over the years, I can only write poems out of my own DNA, much as I want to achieve something akin to the work of poets I admire. I choose my material and methods, but something of what I write was set before I was born. It is my blood, my inher-itance—recognized more than chosen—something to do with that fellow standing where X marks the spot, the fellow who would open up a vanished town and populate it with the living and the dead.

No person is ever really one thing. I am paraphrasing John Donne here, each man a part of the main. Is there a subter-ranean relatedness between us that we too often forget? I am Louis and Luisa, though historians will remind me that Louis was his own man, thank you very much. Zeese Papanikolas tells me the Cretan was probably tougher and more militant than I have made him. Perhaps I have taken some part of him on, some part of the real Louis Tikas, and made use of him as will-fully as I have used the landscape:

This singular man. This footnote nearly lost
from pages of the history books. Louis-
Ilias, named for the fiery prophet,
but often so uncertain of his skin
that only someone else's touch, some whore
who thought he was Sicilian or a Serb,
and took the money first and said no kissing,
made him believe that he was truly alive . . .

What does it mean, nation of immigrants?
What are the accents, fables, voices of roads,
the tall tales told by the smallest desert plants?
Even the wind in barbed wire goads
me into making lines, fencing my vagrant thought.
A story is the language of desire.
A journey home is never what it ought
to be.
         A land of broken glass. Of gunfire.

My own need for intimacy is implicated in what I write—a desire
to be known or understood or simply touched. Writing is a re-
gression to vulnerable states as well as an assertion of powers beyond ourselves. Yet in *Ludlow* I am not merely being confessional. Events did take place. Forces were arrayed in the bloody
American story. People lived and died. David Mason, whoever
the hell he is, forms a very, very small part of the tale.

ฬ

Q: What is a Colorado poet?
A: A poet who lives in Colorado.
Q: What is a Western poet?
A: A poet who lives in the West, especially one born and
raised there.
Q: What is the West?
A: Rivers and mountains and myths.
But I have lived in many places.

I identify at some times with the vanishing self at the crossroads, at others with glaciers and mossy firs, at others with the
Aegean Sea. Like anyone else, I suppose, I know what it means
to shape-shift. I am less than what I love, less than what I admire.

Telling a story, I am related to all storytellers everywhere. Telling it in verse adds a bit of charge, another layer of awareness, and connects my small effort to ancient impulses. A poet is more than a throbbing wound. A poet is also a drummer on the road, trying to open up a town.

# Some Narrative Poets of the American West

Let me tell you a story:

When I was a boy in Bellingham, Washington, a small town on the Puget Sound, closer to Vancouver, B.C., than to Seattle, my family moved to a big house on a hill overlooking the bay. In my teenage years, against my mother's wishes, I would climb out my bedroom window and onto the roof of that house, clamber up to its peak and, clinging to the edge of a brick chimney, look out over the Sound at the San Juan Islands. A would-be writer on my own shingled Parnassus, I thought I lived in a land without poetry, a land no one had written yet. The great writers were elsewhere, Back East or further afield, and I dwelt in a resonant vacancy. Westerners often used to have this feeling—true or not, it seemed our landscapes had not yet found their poets. I dimly knew that someone called Roethke had lived in Seattle, but nothing more about West Coast writers had touched my virgin ears. It would be decades before I read Czeslaw Miłosz's early reaction to the coast, "Far West": "All reputation at last overthrown. / No years, no clocks, no memory of how, kneeling, we panned gold. / The saddles creaked and in the bison grass statues fell apart. / Till there was what was fated. Only the earth and sea."

But there were books in our house. Lots of them. Somehow I stumbled on a small, green paperback anthology, *A Pocket Book of Modern Verse*, edited by Oscar Williams. Among the lines I found there were these: "Here the human past is dim and feeble and alien to us / Our ghosts draw from the crowded future." It seemed true enough. I knew the Lummi Reservation and worked on an archeological dig in a Salish village, but the past here was somehow less culturally sanctioned than that of Greece or Rome or even the Eastern Seaboard of the United States. I read about "This coast crying out for tragedy like all beautiful places. . . ." The voice seemed closer to what I saw from my mother's roof than the impressive Modernism of Pound or Eliot. Out beyond the wide mouth of Bellingham Bay the lights of gillnetters burned all night. The purse seiners motored in from around the point.

> A sudden fog-drift muffled the ocean,
> A throbbing of engines moved in it,
> At length, a stone's throw out, between the rocks and the
> vapor,
> One by one moved shadows
> Out of this mystery, shadows, fishing-boats, trailing each
> other
> Following the cliff for guidance,
> Holding a difficult path between the peril of sea-fog
> And the foam on the shore granite.

I was never far from harbor smells—salt and kelp and creosote. Gulls cried all through my childhood, tides moved, islands and headlands floated between sea and sky.

This poet, Robinson Jeffers, was the first I ever read who expressed something true about the Pacific coast. I found his picture the size of a postage stamp inside the anthology's front cover, and he looked exactly as a poet should—carved out of dreaming stone. He knew my coast. Anyone who grew up as I did, hiking in the Cascades, swimming and sailing in the lakes, tide-pooling at the Sound, would inevitably become an environmentalist of some sort. Human presence in the West was problematic, not the automatic gift some might assume it to be. We knew what silence sounded like—actual silence, uncut by engines of any sort—and it changed us. We never quite got over it or accepted the future crowding in. We lived in a strange imaginative space, not fully named by what we read in books. Jeffers came as close as anyone to that ecology, and later perhaps figures like Kenneth Rexroth, Gary Snyder, John Haines and Robert Hass.

Jeffers was a great lyric poet of the coast who understood the position of humanity in the larger expanse of Nature. That

made sense. Then there were the long narrative poems I began
to find in books, poems with a rough intensity like some of
Faulkner and Lawrence. I didn't understand them. Maybe I still
don't, but they came to represent a level of ambition I rarely saw
in contemporary poetry, as if something essential to the American West could only be captured in the mythologizing impulse
married to the pulse of verse. The first I read was *Roan Stallion,*
with its mixed-race heroine named California and its vivid depiction of wildness, the freedom of riding the great horse and
the imprisonment of human lives. It seemed entirely Western,
but somehow also part of another cosmology, a rush of new
ideas about the place of humanity in the universe, "The atom
bounds-breaking, / Nucleus to sun, electrons to planets, with
recognition / Not praying, self-equaling, the whole to the
whole. . . ." This out-Whitmanned Whitman. The notion that a
woman killing a stallion was also killing God made perfect
sense, though the dramatic arc of the poem felt ever-so-slightly
contrived, driven by idea as much as experience or observation.

Anyone looking at the poetry of the West—and here for the
sake of argument I conflate the deserts west of the Mississippi,
the mountain ranges and the Pacific coast as a vast tract of America sometimes cut off from our cultural centers—will see vari-
eties of narrative verse, ambitious attempts to take in large subjects, large spaces. I'm thinking about Jeffers, but also about
poets like Thomas McGrath, Edward Dorn and W. S. Merwin,
those transplanted generations. To a lesser degree I'm thinking
of three poets born on the West Coast: Dana Gioia, Robert
McDowell and myself. While I cannot hope to be comprehensive
in this brief space, I might add figures as varied as Mark Jarman,
Lawson Inada, Linda McCarriston, Kim Addonizio and Frank
Bidart, some born in the West, some transplanted. Many of us
share a problematic relation to what used to be called the cultural hegemony of the East, where Helen Vendler tells us she
really does not understand narrative poetry, and to certain academic schools that look down upon narrative verse as old-fashioned, insufficiently opaque or otherwise merely human—as if
Modernism had finally rid us of story and we really needn't look
back. Never mind Homer and his lot.

Whatever his faults as a poet, Jeffers presents an example of ambitions we would be poorer without. His foreword to *The Selected Poetry of Robinson Jeffers* (1938) offers ideas that beat against the current of much recent poetry:

> Long ago, before anything included here was written, it became evident to me that poetry—if it was to survive at all—must reclaim of the power and reality that it was so hastily surrendering to prose. . . . It must reclaim substance and sense, and physical and psychological reality. This feeling has been basic in my mind since then. It led me to write narrative poetry, and to draw subjects from contemporary life; to present aspects of life that modern poetry had generally avoided; and to attempt the expression of philosophic and scientific ideas in verse. It was not in my mind to open new fields of poetry, but only to reclaim old freedom.

By itself this isn't a Western phenomenon. Poets as unlike Jeffers as Anthony Hecht and Louis Simpson made similar arguments, and we have the postcolonial example of Derek Walcott's *Omeros* with its pan-African meditations joined to a mock-Homeric narrative. I should also mention the remarkable novel by Vikram Seth, *The Golden Gate,* conveying Bay Area lives with confidence and flair. Contrary to what some critics seem to think, narrative complicates language even as it appears to simplify because it evokes social realities and relationships that are always complex, and because the structures of stories themselves are forms of ambiguity. Narratives are about more than the poet and his or her precious talent. Narratives in verse offer methods of intensification somewhat less available to the prose writer—a *different* way of living in language if not a better one.

So I am claiming Jeffers as one of the great modern proponents of narrative, and I am also claiming a special place for narrative in the West—performing in the twentieth century something of the identity-bearing function narratives by Longfellow, Whittier and others performed in the nineteenth, but also pushing more difficult ideas and a greater variety of forms. Why is it, then, that in truth I sometimes find Jeffers's longer narrative poems less satisfying than his lyrics? Every one of them contains marvelous passages, writing of rare beauty he might not have achieved without the structure and ambition of story. The

problem is sometimes technical. He is not a great writer of dialogue, for example, and his long line does not always seem the
necessary choice for a given passage. But perhaps the problem
of the longer poems is something other than technique, something related to the tragic vision one must bargain with in order
to cross over into belief.

According to Nietzsche, tragedy arises from an essentially religious experience. The song of the suffering being that quavers
between heaven and earth, that most primordial relation of deity
and human, falls into absurdity when we move closer to skeptical
self-consciousness. The primitive religious impulse, throbbing
with violent life, decays into philosophical sophistication.
Aeschylus pulses with tragedy, while Euripides often mocks it. If
many people now have trouble reading some of Jeffers's narratives, perhaps it is because we live in an age of mockery more
than tragedy. We live in what Nietzsche would call a fallen state,
belittling, thwarted by our education, our sophistication, our
irony. When Jeffers gives us the Dionysian horse of *Roan Stallion,*
the incest and sexual energy and violence of his other poems, he
writes out of daemonic impulses few of our contemporaries
share or even understand except at a level of intellectuality.

*Medea* is the most compelling of Jeffers's longer works because
we read it as classical—albeit Euripidean—tragedy. When Medea
says, "I do according to nature what I have to do," we assent to
the cosmology underlying her rationale. Nature is what it is. The
gods are gods, though relatively absent in Jeffers's play. People
are people, and are doomed. All are driven. All are daemonic,
subject to the laws of blood and sex. The brilliant defense of Jeffers made by William Everson (Brother Antoninus) in *Robinson
Jeffers: Fragments of an Older Fury* (1968) notes a "granitic aloof-
ness" in the best of the work, as well as a sensibility alien to literary naturalism. Everson agrees with Frederic Carpenter that the
narrative poems are "modern myths," and points out that we
need to read them differently than we read other storytelling
poems: "For if 'narrative' is the rational ordering of explicit
events and if 'lyric' is the generalization of emotion obtaining
between subject and object, then myths, visions, dreams, are sce-
narios of mood." This abstract sentence attempts to cut a path
into Jeffers's longer poems, acknowledging that this singular

poet cannot be approached in familiar conceptual terms. Since Jeffers himself does little to help with definitions, the burden is on each of us to ask, with Milosz, "What have I to do with you?" A question not easily answered.

As he tells us in "Poetry, Gongorism, and a Thousand Years," Jeffers sought a subject and perspective more durable than the fashions of his time. He believed that ancient Greek tragedies "all tell primitive horror stories, and the conventional pious statements of the chorus are more than balanced by the bad temper and wickedness, or folly, of the principal characters. What makes them noble is the poetry . . ." This is true of the Greeks, but America is a very different society, steeped in melioration even as its citizens can be driven by cutthroat ambition. Nature with a capital N might take the place of the gods, but Jeffers's characters sometimes seem pressed into primitive relation by the author's desire. Maybe this is the point at which our willing suspension of disbelief has to kick in, allowing us to appreciate the intensifying energy of the poems.

Of course this neo-primitivism is one of the major components of the High Modernism Jeffers disliked, characterizing work by Picasso, Stravinsky and Eliot. Combine it with supercharged Freudianism and you get writers like Lawrence and Jeffers. At their best, Jeffers's narratives have a compelling grandeur; at their weakest they feel like tragic contrivances. Mind you, I love a lot of this stuff. Orestes, speaking in *The Tower Beyond Tragedy*, conveys the force of Nature in a manner I recognize:

> I entered the
> life of the brown forest
> And the great life of the ancient peaks, the patience of stone,
> I felt the
> changes in the veins
> In the throat of the mountain, a grain in many centuries, we
> have our own
> time, not yours; and I was the stream
> Draining the mountain wood. . . .

A figure out of the tragic realm, not quite of our time, he adds, "I was mankind also, a moving lichen / On the cheek of the rounded stone. . . ." Jeffers wants us to feel again an animal relation to the world. He wants us, as all the best poets do, to be more than intellect, more than our timid selves clinging to cultural assurances. He wants us to be exposed to more life than we can bear.

I think of the great descriptive set pieces in a poem like *Cawdor*—that caged eagle killing a squirrel, or the marine life of the coast, or this passage when the old man finds a piece of chipped flint:

> Cawdor picked up the Indian-wrought stone. "There were
>     people here before us," he said, "and others will come
> After our time. These poor flints were their knives, wherever
>     you dig you find them, and now I forget
> What we came up for."

In other words, whatever his flaws as a storyteller, however unaccommodating his tragic vision may seem, Jeffers was onto something. There really is a human relation to the world that we need to work through in our poetry, whether it is understood in scientific, political or religious terms. Everson also read Jeffers in the light of the American Transcendentalist tradition, referring to "the long, somber and God-tormented poems" and how they suited "our fundamental native pantheism." The "grandeur and scale" of Jeffers's narratives make demands we are not always willing to meet, but they also present an example we should not reject. Poems that tell stories involve readers in larger communal structures, dramas beyond ourselves without which poetry is a terribly diminished art. Finding sympathy for what seems alien to us is one of poetry's major functions.

Jeffers remains a great poet, though perhaps antithetical to New Critical readings—I say this knowing that Everson and others have read him very closely. The poets he influenced are also mavericks of one sort or another, many of them still marginalized. One of these mavericks was Thomas McGrath, known to some as a communist poet who never outgrew a 1930s mindset, but to others as an important wordsmith, author of the fascinating long poem *Letter to an Imaginary Friend*. While McGrath's early influences included such leftist poets as Auden, MacNeice and Brecht, he was in some sense a regionalist—he grew up in North Dakota, served in the Aleutians during World War II, was blacklisted in California—and came of age when Jeffers's reputation was still at its height. McGrath told an interviewer that in the 1930s, "I blundered across Jeffers. He wasn't turning up in the anthologies yet. But I blundered across him, then I read and read him." McGrath did not share Jeffers's isolationist politics, but was attracted by the long lines and richly modulated rhythms as well as the Western landscapes. There was also the affinity of one provincial poet for another. Jeffers had chosen his Monterrey coast after a privileged upbringing, while McGrath grew up in what seemed an unwritten terrain. Both poets were career outsiders, utterly individual in their stance, in many ways removed from the literary establishment.

*Letter to an Imaginary Friend* is not a narrative poem in the way Jeffers wrote mythic stories. Rather, it is a visionary autobiography, its leftist politics and Native American theology implying a new poetic DNA. It pleads a revolution in consciousness, an improved world in ironic contrast to the political one in which we dwell. But many of the strongest passages in McGrath's poem are narrative set pieces, and his long line clearly owes something to Jeffers. I think of McGrath's early Virgil figure, a farmhand named Cal who, as a Wobbly, guides the young Tom toward political awareness. Tom's uncle hates these leftist agitators, and gives Cal a severe beating:

> Cal spoke for the men and my uncle cursed him.
> I remember that ugly sound, like some animal cry touching
>     me
> Deep and cold, and I ran toward them
> And the fighting started.
> My uncle punched him. I heard the breaking crunch
> Of his teeth going and the blood leaped out of his mouth
> Over his neck and shirt—I heard their gruntings and
>     strainings
> Like love at night or men working hard together,
> And heard the meaty thumpings, like beating a grain sack
> As my uncle punched his body—I remember the dust
> Jumped from his shirt.

In the wake of this violence, upsetting to everyone in McGrath's family, the boy runs off alone to the Sheyenne River. There, among the trees, "Runeless I stood in the green rain / Of the leaves." He seeks a kind of solace in Nature, which Jeffers would understand even as he knew how unforgiving Nature could be.

McGrath differs from Jeffers partly in his revolutionary politics, but also in his sense of humor. In Part II of *Letter* a long scene of Catholic confession could have come right out of James Joyce:

> "Well, boy?"
> "I think I deserve a harder penance, Father."
> "Such as?"
> "As among the Spiritual Works of Mercy, Father:
> To instruct the ignorant. To admonish sinners."
> "It takes one to
> know one.
> What else?"
> "As among the Corporeal Works of Mercy, Father:
> To bury the dead. To visit those in prison."
> "All in time.
> For now: three Our Fathers and three Hail Marys. Hop to it!"
> It's less than I can face. "There's more, Father there's more!"
> "Then spit it out and get on with it yez, y'little spalpeen!"
>
> But what's the more to get on to? I call upon all the words
> In the dictionary of damnation and not a damned one will
> come.
> I pray for the gift of tongues and suddenly I am showered
> With all the unknown words I have ever heard or read.
>
> "I am guilty of chrestomathy, Father."
> He lets out a grunt in
> Gaelic,
> Shifting out of the Latin to get a fresh purchase on sin.
> "And?"
> "Barratry, Father
> "And mineralogy . . .
> "Agatism and summer elements . . .
> "Skepticism about tooth fairies . . .
> "Catachresis and pseudogogy . . .
> "I have poisoned poissons in all the probable statistics . . .
> "I have had my pidgin and eaten it too, Father . . ."

McGrath was fully capable of spoiling a poem with political piety. What saves him at his best is the "sin" of language love, an understanding of poetry as play, far from the dourness of his fellow Celt Jeffers. But of course McGrath wrote in the wake of World War II and Korea, during the American misadventure in Vietnam, a time when pieties of all sorts were increasingly suspect.

To move even further from Jeffers, perhaps no one was less the tragedian than Edward Dorn in *Gunslinger*, part pop-epic, part script for performance with guitar. A series of punning riffs on myths of the West, *Gunslinger* is so arch, so auto-reflexive, that it nearly demolishes such distinctions as character and story. Slinger is part daemon, part dime-novel, a son of the sun, a fading force in a bullet-riddled, ahistorical desert. A poet figure tells the story, such as it is, and acts in constant dialogue with Slinger and his talking, dope-smoking Horse. Like some dislodged syllable of Rimbaud, the poet is named simply "I." One quickly realizes that *Gunslinger* exists for its anarchy, closer to Laurence Sterne than to Robinson Jeffers. In an introduction to a new edition, Marjorie Perloff says that *Gunslinger* "marks an important turning point in American poetry, a turn away from the monologic lyric of mid-century to the dialogic 'parapoem' of fin de siècle, with its amalgam of 'theory' and lyric, of prose narrative and sound-text, and especially of citation embedded in or superimposed upon the speech of a particular self."

She makes it sound like a panel discussion at the MLA, but the book is much more fun than that. I bring it up because it is a long poem of the American West. Though born in Illinois and with formative ties to the Black Mountain School and England, Dorn spent important years in Washington State and died in Colorado. *Gunslinger* shares with the narratives of Jeffers and McGrath a deliberate outsider status that owes something to the landscape as well as the languages of the West:

> Cool flight along our trail
> comes a rupture of feathers,
> Laterally comes the desert lark
> throat of memory of an extinct tree
> into the light of afterdark
> gone out to the dry sea in bateaux

Cool dry,
Shall come the results of inquiry
out of the larks throat
oh people of the coming stage
out of the larks throat
loom the hoodoos
beyond the canyon country
Oh temptation of survival
oh lusterless hope
of victory in opposites

Dorn saw the West as a place where old mythologies go to die. What survives is language, I suppose, and the way he laces Spanish idiom into some of his lines reminds me of a very different mythologizer of the West: Cormac McCarthy. While I know Jeffers influenced McGrath and Merwin and my own generation, I do not know quite why it is that critics have sometimes paired Jeffers and Dorn except for this interest in the West. Dorn has been quoted praising Jeffers's elegance as a poet, and he must have been attracted to the risky ambition of narratives set in a place still largely unsanctioned by literary criticism.

One more example. W. S. Merwin came to the West and overshot it to the Pacific isles of Hawaii. By the time he made this move he had already established himself as a prodigious talent in such cultural centers as Boston and New York, and had lived yet another life in France and Spain. His devotion to narrative poetry looks back at least to medieval Europe, a subject on which he was expert while a very young man. What distinguishes *The Folding Cliffs* (1998) from the other narratives I have mentioned here is that its presiding spirit is neither tragic nor satirical, nor is it purely political. Merwin shares the Western writer's sympathy for Native Americans (think of Jeffers's poem "Hands" and McGrath's use of Hopi religion). He understands that the story of the West is in part a story of displacement, even genocide. The poet opposes the amnesia of the dominant culture. The story he tells about the near-eradication of native culture in Hawaii is in that sense a common one for our country, a poetic addendum to Dee Brown's *Bury My Heart at Wounded Knee*.

In an interview Merwin stated that he disagreed with Jeffers's nihilism, "a kind of hugging to himself of a bitterness which really, I thought, in the long run, was egocentric." What Merwin admired, though, was the ecology of Jeffers, the effort to "uncenter our minds from ourselves," as Jeffers put it in "Carmel Point." Still something of a humanist, Merwin tells his Hawaiian story with sensitivity for a variety of people, native and white. He has a novelist's eye for manners and a scientist's interest in the Nature lying beyond them. But there is also the ecologist at work in this poem. After an opening section introducing his major characters, he suddenly reverts to geological time, the fiery birth of the islands:

> The mountain rises by itself out of the turning night
> > out of the floor of the sea and is the whole of an
> > > island
> alone in the one horizon alone in the entire day
> > as a word is alone in the moment it is spoken
> meaning what it means only then and meaning it only
> > once with the same syllables that have arisen
> and have formed and been uttered before again and again

Language and storytelling, human memory itself—these things arise in almost mystical relation to the landscape, as if the folding cliffs were the lobes of memory and human culture might have at its core a genuineness, an essence modern man has forgotten. Surely Jeffers would have recognized such beliefs. My point is not that they are true—since they cannot really be proven—but that they are endemic to American animism or Transcendentalism, so rife in the West.

But now the future has crowded in. I have strayed far from Jeffers to suggest glancing relations to a variety of narratives. The West now has plenty of poets, from rappers to post-structuralists, and remains, like most of America, an amnesiac culture. The grandeur of Jeffers can seem out of place to contemporary readers shy of big emotions, but it will be lodged there as an example if we keep reminding people to read him. Read him for the flawed poet he is, for the beautiful lyrics as well as the tortured narratives, examples we need but do not always agree with. Art is not a matter of agreement, after all, but recognition. The same sensibility that can make a narrative feel forced or over the top can position us precisely in meditative space:

Below us, and under our feet
The heavy black stones of the cairn of the Lord of Ulster.
A man of blood who died bloodily
Four centuries ago: but death's nothing, and life,
From a high death-mark on a headland
Of this dim island of burials, is nothing either.
How beautiful are both these nothings.

This is poetry open to contradiction and impurity, built from an unfashionable belief in lasting things—or relatively lasting things, since of course "man will be blotted out, the blithe earth die, the brave sun / Die blind and blacken to the heart. . . ."

Poets who tell stories admit that we are in this together, that individual talent is not enough. Our anger and grief can be shared. We have other examples before us, more than I can list here, but I doubt any of us would have attempted quite what we have done without the audacity of Robinson Jeffers.

# Modern American Poetry and the
# Hopper of Civilization

One beats and beats for that which one believes.
That's what one wants to get near.
 —Wallace Stevens, "The Man on the Dump"

American muse, whose strong and diverse heart
So many men have tried to understand
But only made it smaller with their art. . . .
 —Stephen Vincent Benét, *John Brown's Body*

The first great American poet of the twentieth century was almost completely unknown when the century began. In fact, Edwin Arlington Robinson was temporarily rescued from abject poverty by none other than the president of the United States, Theodore Roosevelt, who had been given *The Children of the Night* by his son Kermit. He not only invited Robinson to the White House for a lengthy chat, but reviewed his book and found a job for him as "a special agent of the Treasury" in the New York Custom House. Robert Mezey's introduction to *The Poetry of E. A. Robinson* (Modern Library, 1999) explains, "It was understood by everyone that this was a sinecure; Robinson's job was to write poetry. He went to the Custom House every morning, read the newspaper, folded it neatly on his desk, and left. I cannot think of another American president who has been so disinterestedly generous to a great writer."

Nor can I. While it is true that Teddy Roosevelt displayed questionable taste in the Robinson poems he singled out for praise, the very fact that he *willingly read the poets of his time and declared what his tastes were* is astonishing. Many editors of the day considered Robinson too dark and pessimistic for their readers; his work already included such poems as "Luke Havergal,"

"Richard Cory," "Reuben Bright" and the villanelle called "The House on the Hill":

> There is ruin and decay
>   In the House on the Hill:
> They are all gone away,
> There is nothing more to say.

Whatever the hell poetry was, some editors believed, it shouldn't disturb our sleep! Yet what made Robinson great was not only his pessimism, but also his mordant humor and penetrating sense of character. He modernized diction and syntax in his measured lines without the benefit of an Ezra Pound. Though his worst poems do sound stilted today, Robinson's best can stand with just about anyone's. His story is instructive because the best poet at the turn of our own new century is quite possibly someone whose work we do not know, and of whom the critics have not yet expressed their approval. I very much doubt that the 2000 election will provide us with a president who could bring such a poet's work to light.

Robinson was also a man who, though part of no movement or clique, thought about what it meant to be an American poet:

> I am just beginning to fully realize that America is the hopper through which the whole civilization of the world is to be ground—consciously or otherwise. I am not much of an American, either—in a popular way; but I am glad to feel an inkling as to what the western continent was made for.

It seems a remarkably prescient comment in some ways. Immigration quotas were up (except for Asian applicants), and even early in the century one could see that America was absorbing the spillage of world cultures like a giant sponge. As Robinson perused and folded his newspaper, American poetry was poised to expand in directions few could have anticipated, and it would continue to harvest whatever was planted, or transplanted, in American soil (to say nothing of Americans who transplanted themselves elsewhere). However, Robinson's hopper metaphor is also rather disturbing; it could imply that, sooner or later, we'll shuck the distinctiveness from those many cultures, funnel them down and reduce them to bleached flour. As much as American culture was in the twentieth century a vital force on the planet, I sympathize with some resistance to it. Robinson might have sympathized too: "I am not much of an American, either—in a popular way." Whatever American poetry becomes, it will have to contain *le Big Mac* as well as "Le Monocle de Mon Oncle," just as surely as Langston loved the blues and Old Possum sang "The Shakespearean Rag."

꒰ꢲ

When commentators from other countries look at America now, they declare that we are experiencing a poetry renaissance. Perhaps it is true. There are sometimes large audiences for poetry slams and readings. Many new books are published (though many fewer are actually read). Bushels of prizes are handed out, April's cruelty now includes National Poetry Month, and in a few cities poems appear on public transportation. Poems adorn our culture like wreaths on public statues, though we're usually too busy and distracted to notice them. Robert Pinsky's "favorite poem" videos are a genuine contribution—and other poets laureate have made their contributions, hoping popularity will do the art some good. But a renaissance is supposed to produce and then celebrate masterpieces, and I am not confident that ours will do so. After all, the major newspapers and magazines too rarely review new books of poems, and when they do they choose the usual anointed mediocrities. How boring it is, and how offputting for any real audience, that the same poets are mentioned over and over again in those rare prominent reviews, and that such mention has nothing to do with whether or not their books are any good. The chain bookstores dress their poetry sections with some of the anointed, and also the anointed of previous generations in old editions with bright new covers. The journals and Web sites proliferate. And the truly wonderful poems—poems with unforgettable lines that move or chill or intrigue us—are as rare as they ever were. Some renaissance.

In 1870, William Cullen Bryant produced *The Library of World Poetry*, a very ambitious compendium, declaring, "It is to be hoped that every reader of this collection, however he may have been trained, will find in the great variety of its contents something conformable to his taste." Now the editors of the Library of America have conceived *American Poetry: The Twentieth Century* along related lines. Two out of four projected volumes have been published. Volume 1 is 986 pages long; volume 2 is 1009 (I tried counting the poets but kept losing my place). *American Poetry: The Nineteenth Century* took up two weighty volumes, impressively edited by John Hollander. For the twentieth century a committee of advisors has been assembled (in addition to Hollander it includes Robert Hass, Carolyn Kizer, Nathaniel Mackay and Marjorie Perloff). I wonder if there is a correlation between these numbers and editorial sprawl. Imagine an anthology of the twenty-first century taking up eight volumes—the thing would be suitable only for jacking up houses or starting riots.

Another problem is that of official sanction; the very idea of a Library of America anthology implies that all these poets have been stuffed and put on display. Poets included so far were born between 1838 and 1913. Just imagine how much trouble the next volumes will give the committee, starting with someone like Weldon Kees, William Stafford, John Berryman or Randall Jarrell (all born in 1914) and coming forward to poets born in the fifties and later, poets who are still playing a desperate and discordant game of musical chairs for a place in the canon. How will this committee (or another, if it takes that long) decide who gets to sit down and who must keep on dancing?

If I would argue that these editors have erred on the side of inclusiveness, I would also admit that I can't see the project going any other way, though I would differ in degree. I like the fact that our first encounter in volume 1 is with Anonymous Ballads. It's especially witty that they begin with "White House Blues," occasioned by the assassination of William McKinley by an anarchist named Leon Czolgosz—an event that put Teddy Roosevelt in the White House. Both volumes place poets side by side with songwriters, including such figures as W. C. Handy, Joe Hill, Ma Rainey, Irving Berlin, Cole Porter, Bessie Smith, Oscar Hammerstein II, Lorenz Hart, Ira Gershwin, Blind Lemon Jefferson, Johnny Mercer, Frank Loesser, Woody Guthrie and Lightnin' Hopkins. Both volumes include poems by writers we usually associate with other genres, like Henry Adams and Edith Wharton.

Adams's poem is included for historical significance, as it arose in part from his famous walk through the hall of dynamos at the Paris World's Fair in 1900; it signals us that machines would be important to writers of the period. Soon after this we find Harriet Monroe's enjoyable period piece "Radio," followed by the frankly passionate Wharton poem "Terminus," both of which signal the very real importance of women's voices. We also have two poems by W. E. B. DuBois, usually thought of as a great editor, social critic and historian—another signal, this time that the anthology will be sensitive to issues of race.

None of the above-mentioned poems achieves anything like greatness; each is included for some constituency. Early in volume 1 we also find an excerpt from "The Poet in the Desert," by Charles Erskin Scott Wood (1852–1944), and have occasion to be grateful for the biographical notes in the back despite their broken prose. Wood's poem, first published in 1915, the same year Eliot's "Prufrock" and "Preludes" appeared in print, is pretty dull and prosaic. His life, on the other hand, was nothing of the sort:

> Appointed in 1869 to U.S. Military Academy at West Point, where career was marked by numerous infractions of discipline. Commissioned as second lieutenant in 1874 and joined 21st infantry in California. Worked as surveyor in northern California; served as judge advocate of the department of the Columbia. Relieved from active military duty in 1877 to join Taylor expedition to Alaska, of which he assumed leadership. Served in campaigns against Nez Percé Indians in 1877 and against Bannock and Piute, 1878; appointed aide-de-camp to General Oliver Otis Howard. Married Nannie Moale Smith in 1879. Entered Columbia University in 1881, where he met sculptor Olin Warner and painter Albert Pinkerton Ryder; after graduating, returned to active military duty in Boise City, Idaho. Resigned from army in March 1884 after threat of court-martial; began successful legal practice in Portland, Oregon. Helped found Portland Art Association in 1888. . . .

It goes on, spectacularly, connecting Wood to Emma Goldman, John Cowper Powys, Robinson Jeffers and others. He even gets fingered by the House Un-American Activities Committee—the guy was *everywhere*. So what if his poem hardly bears reading—his biography certainly does.

In other words, the first principle for editing this anthology was historical, and it was presumed that poems would be included not because they were masterpieces of the art, but because they represented some idea or trend or readership. This makes for very dull reading in a number of places. However, it also gives us a rather rich and complicated portrait of the age. These Library of America anthologies are documentary histories more than poetry books, which makes it even worse that they don't date individual poems, allowing us to chart careers and trends more precisely. While I hope that someone will provide us one day with an anthology half as long and containing only good poems, I can also recognize the need for a book such as this one, a curiosity of political and literary scholarship.

There is plenty of eccentricity here, from proto–Cowboy Poets like Badger Clark and Roy Helton to Elsa von Freytag-Loringhoven, whose poetry reminds me of an old woman I once saw in the bowels of Grand Central Station, dressed in a grimy slip and muttering incoherently to some imaginary auditor. Freytag-Loringhoven, however, is pure pleasure next to the long-winded pretensions of Gertrude Stein in "Lifting Belly" (I'll spare you quotations, but direct you to Helen Vendler's incisive review in the *New Republic,* June 19, 2000). It is fair to say that, as necessary as Modernism was, it produced a lot of lousy poetry. One has to look pretty hard to find the good lines in Mina Loy's work, and few of Pound's *Cantos* seem compelling anymore. Eugene Jolas appears to have taken the term "pig Latin" rather too seriously, while Abraham Lincoln Gillespie's "A Purplexicon of Dissynthegrations" is perplexing without being graceful, and Ramon Guthrie's "Elegy for Mélusine from the Intensive Care Ward" is about as moving as a shot of sodium pentothal. I have other questions, too. Why include so many of Charles Reznikoff's poems imitating journal entries, so few of his poems imitating poems? Why so much Genevieve Taggard? Why Lynn Riggs? Why a fragment from Dos Passos's *U.S.A.*, as if it were a poem? Why the weak poems of Robert Hillyer, Edmund Wilson, Isidor Schneider, Emanuel Carnevali? Why so much Léonie Adams and why any Hildegarde Flanner? Carl Rakoski is another

whose life is more interesting than his work, and Louis Zukof-
sky's selections could have been trimmed, to say the least. Here's
a fragment of his *Poem beginning "The"*:

1 The
2 Voice of Jesus I. Rush singing
3                              in the wilderness
4 A boy's best friend is his mother,
5 It's your mother all the time.
6 Residue of Oedipus wrecks
7 Creating out of the dead,—
8 From the candle flames of the souls of dead mothers. . . .

And it goes on, like a maze of footnotes. If I'm going to lose my
eyesight, let it be over lines that lift me to a new level of consciousness, not lines that put me to sleep. In the avant-garde
poems that I do enjoy, I usually discover the most archaic
virtues, lyricism or narrative. But it's not just "experimental" poetry that gags me in these volumes. Why do we have lame poems
like Howard Baker's "Advice to a Man Who Lost a Dog"? What
is meant by including John Wheelwright's "Fish Food: An Obit-
uary to Hart Crane," which reads like a parody gone wrong?

> The sea's teats have suckled you, and you are sunk far
> in bubble dreams, under swaying translucent vines
> of thundering interior wonder. . . .

And yes, I would also like to know why there is so little narrative poetry in these volumes, especially when many pages are
taken up with pretentious babbling. The editors cannot hon-
estly say that narrative poems are too long to be included under
such circumstances. Why do we get a fragment of Joseph
March's *The Wild Party*, but not a single narrative by Jeffers? We
get one narrative of Robinson, more from Frost, Bishop's "Cru-
soe in England," but that's about it. Obviously there was a reaction against narrative among Modernist poets, but that didn't
quash it altogether. There is also some inconsistency in the way
these volumes build upon Hollander's anthology of the nineteenth century. Why, for example, does Edith Wharton appear
in both centuries while Paul Laurence Dunbar does not? And

why do the editors of the new volumes leave out some of Robinson's best early poems just because they were first published in the 1890s? Readers who buy only the twentieth-century volumes will wonder what became of those well-known Robinson poems I praised at the beginning of this review. I could go on and on, listing the shortcomings of the project and its broadly historical design, but I confess that the anthology also contains surprises, as well as an opportunity to reacquaint oneself with the major poets of the period.

&#158;

Which raises another question: just who were the major poets? I'm afraid that my own list is fairly traditional: E. A. Robinson, Robert Frost, Wallace Stevens, William Carlos Williams, Ezra Pound (minus most of the *Cantos*), T. S. Eliot, Robinson Jeffers, Marianne Moore and (the only candidate I would pick from volume 2) e. e. cummings. I should also list Theodore Roethke and Elizabeth Bishop, both of whom left behind marvelous poems. None of these writers is invulnerable to criticism, of course. I think Frost is the greatest of the bunch, but I wouldn't want to live in a world in which all poetry was like Frost's. The selection of his work here is very, very good, including the great dramatic narratives like "Home Burial" and "The Witch of Coös." The latter is an eerie comic masterpiece; just look at the description of a murdered man's skeleton clambering up from a farmhouse basement:

> It left the cellar forty years ago
> And carried itself like a pile of dishes
> Up one flight from the cellar to the kitchen,
> Another from the kitchen to the bedroom,
> Another from the bedroom to the attic,
> Right past both father and mother, and neither stopped it.
> Father had gone upstairs; mother was downstairs.
> I was a baby: I don't know where I was.

As he does in "Home Burial," Frost unobtrusively offers an image of a domestic power-struggle in terms of the physical placement of each of his principal characters. Both poems have a kind of horror at the core, but in "The Witch of Coös" we can laugh as well as shudder. The anthology also includes great meditations like "After Apple-Picking" and "Birches," "Two Tramps in Mud Time" and "Directive." One could wish for more—"The Black Cottage," for example, a poem that reminds me of Maupassant's "Mother Savage"—but with more than sixty pages, the Frost selection is bountiful enough. There are also his extraordinary lyrics, from the early "Mowing" to "Come In." I closed these volumes confirmed in my belief that Frost wrote more truthfully and memorably than any other American poet. He never wrote about urban and suburban life, but that's like complaining that Dante never played Vegas.

Stevens, with his "Forms, flames and the flakes of flames," is an almost constant delight. Look at the ending of his poem "The Man on the Dump":

> Is it peace,
> Is it a philosopher's honeymoon, one finds
> On the dump? Is it to sit among mattresses of the dead,
> Bottles, pots, shoes and grass and murmur *aptest eve:*
> Is it to hear the blatter of grackles and say
> *Invisible priest;* is it to eject, to pull
> The day to pieces and cry *stanza my stone?*
> Where was it one first heard of the truth? The the.

Stevens was often the philosopher on holiday, though rarely in a state of peace. He mouthed words in primal pleasure. (Why is it I always want to recite "The Emperor of Ice Cream" with a W. C. Fields accent?) I can't help missing some poems: "Bantams in Pine Woods," "The Anecdote of the Jar," "The Man Whose Pharynx Was Bad," "To the Roaring Wind," "The Sense of the Sleight-of-hand Man," "Of Modern Poetry" and "Metamorphosis." I wish they had given us "Esthétique du Mal" instead of the complete *Notes Toward a Supreme Fiction*. What can I do but demur and move on?

I love Pound for his irascibility, the sheer vitality of his voice: that woman "dying piece-meal / of a sort of emotional anaemia" who "is almost afraid" that he will speak to her; or his succinctness in "Hugh Selwyn Mauberley" when he says, "The age demanded an image / Of its accelerated grimace. . . ." In Parts IV and V of that poem he captured the insanity of World War I as well as any writer ever did, and with stunning brevity. I love Williams for the vernacular voice he invented, and I wish his "Tract" and "Death" were included, the selections from *Paterson* cut. Both of these pioneering writers left a residue of combative personality behind, a more memorable stance toward life than I find in their imitators. In Robinson Jeffers, even in the too-small selection offered here, there is a rare grandeur:

> This coast crying out for tragedy, like all beautiful places:
>     and like the passionate spirit of humanity
> Pain for its bread: God's, many victims', the painful deaths,
>     the horrible transfigurements: I said in my heart,
> "Better invent than suffer: imagine victims
> Lest your own flesh be chosen the agonist, or you
> Martyr some creature to the beauty of this place."

It was Jeffers who gave voice to the coast where Frost had spent his childhood. Though Frost was the greater poet, Jeffers lifts us to places that Frost was too much the ironist to approach. And take a look at how deliberate a thinker he is in "Advice to Pilgrims": "That our senses lie and our minds trick us is true, but in general / They are honest rustics; trust them a little. . . ."

Though I feel about Marianne Moore as I do about most other poets, that she is best taken in small doses, what delectable doses she left us. Who else would say this to a steam roller: "You lack half wit. You crush all particles down / into close conformity, and then walk back and forth on them." If Moore never moves me deeply, her intelligent edge nevertheless has its poetry. Ultimately, I agree with Randall Jarrell that her protégé, Elizabeth Bishop, became a more satisfying poet with a more physical sense of experience than Moore. Because she planted herself bodily in her poems, Bishop seems to me closer to Frost and Hemingway than to other American writers. She is represented by nineteen poems in the present anthology, and I re-read them without yawning once. Anne Stevenson has pointed out Bishop's indebtedness to Darwin in the way she observes the world, and the fine surfaces of her poems are made even finer by the injured, stoical humanity that underlies them.

Each of the poets I have called "great" is in some way eccentric. None more so than e. e. cummings, for obvious reasons.

Cummings is often remembered for cuteness—the "puddle-wonderful" world and all that. But his best poems do what the best poems always do—they provide us with a new level of alertness, sometimes by estrangement, sometimes by familiarity. They are vital objects, and they say a thing as well as it can be said. I like his outrage in "POEM, OR BEAUTY HURTS MR. VINAL":

> I do however protest,anent the un
> -spontaneous and otherwise scented merde which
> greets one(Everywhere Why)as divine poesy per
> that and this radically defunct periodical.

I like the way he playfully renews the ballad subject matter in "anyone lived in a pretty how town," and the sad psychological accuracy of "my father moved through dooms of love." Cummings was a classic love poet who had an utterly original way of breaking and rebuilding words and syntax. The editors of this anthology were right to give him plenty of pages. Against his vitality I might place the sickness of T. S. Eliot, a sort of American Baudelaire. I do not always love Eliot's poetry, yet I find it in places unforgettable. I resent the effect he had on critics and subsequent poets—the excessive allusiveness, the footnoting, the precious exegeses, the dissertations that make me wonder if we shouldn't scrap all English departments and start fresh. He may very well be a dead end in American poetry, but unlike so many of his imitators, Eliot wrote lines of uncanny fascination and power. His was a singularly rigorous example in both prose and verse, and we shall be wrestling with his work for a long time to come.

Poetry is a subject of study, and I do not wish to suggest that I am anti-intellectual, only that study is but part of the matter, pleasure a great deal more. Possibly here I differ with Helen Vendler, who seems indifferent to "lighter" kinds of poetry and yearns to anthologize only masterpieces—something she did not manage to do in her *Harvard Book of Contemporary American Poetry*. Bryant was able to recognize that "to the great mass of mankind poetry is really a delight and a refreshment. To many, perhaps to most, it is not requisite that it should be of the highest degree of merit." My own preferences fall somewhere between the two institutional thinkers. I've already enumerated bits of what I would have cut from the Library of America volumes. I should end by listing more of what I am happy to find.

First of all, I'm glad to find poets who are very good but not quite great, like Edgar Lee Masters, Elinor Wylie, Edna St. Vincent Millay, John Crowe Ransom, Hart Crane, Archibald MacLeish, Dorothy Parker, Rolfe Humphries, Karl Shapiro, Delmore Schwartz, Thomas Hornsby Ferril, Louise Bogan, Stephen Vincent Benét, Yvor Winters, Janet Lewis, Sterling Brown, Ogden Nash, Robert Francis, Lorine Niedecker, Stanley Kunitz, George Oppen, Kenneth Rexroth, Constance Carrier and no doubt others who have slipped my mind. That's a bumpy road of names behind me now, with highs and lows of various kinds. I look forward to the day when literary critics can take stock of the fact that Yvor Winters and Kenneth Rexroth were both important poets of the West, that J. V. Cunningham's "To What Strangers, What Welcome" is a bona fide American masterpiece, that Allen Tate could be a real bore but left behind two or three strong poems. I'm glad these anthologists included all of Robert Penn Warren's "Audubon: A Vision" (which, come to think of it, adds to the number of narrative poems), and I'm happy to find poets like Robert Fitzgerald and Mary Barnard. It's good that we get a large dose of Robert Hayden, surely one of the best poets of his generation, and that we are allowed to see how John Reed (in one poem) and Kenneth Fearing (in several) provided at least as much outrage as Ginsberg before "Howl" came along. I also feel that a little H. D. goes a long way, and the same goes for Amy Lowell and Carl Sandburg. And I could have used more John Frederick Nims, though the one poem they give us is beautiful. Franklin Adams is more fun than Henry, Don Marquis a delight. Witter Bynner and Arthur Davison Ficke were at their best in the Spectra hoax, when they impersonated Imagists. I wish Countee Cullen had lived longer and extended his arguments about form with Langston Hughes. I learn that Vachel Lindsay had probably the most horrible death of all the poets here— suicide by swallowing Lysol—and that when she learned of it, Sara Teasdale took her own overdose of sleeping pills. The Communist Max Eastman found the perfect cover as "a contributing editor of *Reader's Digest*." Carl Rakoski once worked "as psychologist for Bloomingdale's." What characters!

Ultimately, the various movements in modern American poetry mean less than the triumph of a few poets and the fine individual poems written by many others. In the next volumes, whenever they arrive, we will find Bishop's friends—Robert Lowell et al.—and then the generation born in the 1920s, including Wilbur, Hecht, Justice, Rich, Simpson and Ginsberg. No doubt a multicultural emphasis will grow stronger, just as it has historically, with a similar mixture of right and wrongheadedness. And it will be harder than ever to separate the wheat from the chaff.

# The Long and the
# Short of Robinson

May we who are alive be slow
To tell what we shall never know.
—E. A. Robinson, "Exit"

The best poets are often eccentrics of one sort or another. They have to get used to being misunderstood. So it has been with Edwin Arlington Robinson, who died in 1935, one of the most popular and laureled authors of his time after decades of obscurity, now fallen to semi-obscurity again. He began self-publishing at a bad time for American poetry, the 1890s, living to see the renaissance associated with Modernism and the rise of new periodicals like *Poetry,* established in 1912. Yet Robinson remained on the margins of fashion, closer in manner to Thomas Hardy and Robert Frost than to the ornamentation of William Vaughan Moody, on the one hand, or the mandarin style of T. S. Eliot on the other.

While Robinson has never left the anthologies—not the good ones, anyway—he remains a poet in need of periodic resuscitation, usually by poet-critics of particular discernment. Recent selections of his work by Donald Hall and Robert Mezey have been welcomed and, in the latter case, allowed by irresponsible publishers to go out of print. Robert Faggen's fair selection for Penguin remains available, and now we have an Everyman pocket edition by Scott Donaldson, who performs another service in his thorough new biography of the poet, *Edwin Arlington Robinson: A Poet's Life.* The fact that this first-rate literary biography appears under a university imprint is further evidence, if any were needed, that commercial publishers have lost their bearings. But at least the book exists and is getting some attention. Robinson deserves it.

Donaldson's many books include biographies of Hemingway, Fitzgerald and Cheever, as well as poets Archibald MacLeish and Winfield Townley Scott. The new book displays a particular affinity for poetry—and the way poems survive through small acts of generosity. His introduction tells us that W. S. Merwin recently demonstrated such devotion by reciting "Reuben Bright" from memory at a Paris bookstore, prompted when he faltered briefly by another poet in the room. Donaldson uses the occasion to move beyond that one great sonnet to the elusive subject of voice:

> Great writers must find their distinctive voice, and you can hear Robinson in "Reuben Bright" (1897). He uses simple rhetoric, the emotion compressed in spare language. As the poet Winfield Townley Scott observed in his notebooks, there are basically two kinds of poetry. One is represented by Hart Crane's line "The seal's wide spindrift gaze toward paradise," the other by Robinson's "And he was all alone there when he died." One is a magic gesture of language, the other "a commentary on human life so concentrated as to give off considerable pressure." The greatest poets combine the two, Scott believed: Shakespeare often, Robinson himself now and then.

I have rarely encountered a more useful critical observation, illuminating not only the level of Robinson's contribution, but also two effective poetic modes.

Robinson was one of the first *modern* American poets. When we read him merely as a social realist with a penchant for the lower depths we miss a more challenging quality in his voice, a sportive freedom of association almost between the lines. Notice, for example, the verbal play typical of Wallace Stevens, born a decade after Robinson, in 1879. This is "To the Roaring Wind," the final poem of *Harmonium* (1923):

> What syllable are you seeking,
> Vocalissimus,
> In the distances of sleep?
> Speak it.

Now look at Robinson's equally goofy and delightful poem "Two Men" from 1897:

> There be two men of all mankind
>     That I should like to know about;
> But search and question where I will,
>     I cannot ever find them out.
>
> Melchizedek, he praised the Lord
>     And gave some wine to Abraham;
> But who can tell what else he did
>     Must be more learned than I am.
>
> Ucalegon, he lost his house
>     When Agamemnon came to Troy;
> But who can tell me who he was—
>     I'll pray the gods to give him joy.
>
> There be two men of all mankind
>     That I'm forever thinking on:
> They chase me everywhere I go,—
>     Melchizedek, Ucalegon.

I suppose one could dissertate about the two cultural strands of Greek and Hebrew, or go on about Robinson's obsession with lives that would barely inhabit other poets' footnotes, but it's the quality of play I want most to stress here, the delight in saying the syllables and the anarchy of laughter in that final line. Neither of these poems represents the best work by either poet, yet both display a slippery irreverence close to the spirit of the art.

Frost had this irreverence too, a great poet who comes off rather badly as a man—mean-spirited and competitive—in Donaldson's biography. Asked to introduce Robinson's last, posthumously published book, *King Jasper,* Frost grudgingly rose to the occasion and in the end produced one of his best essays, wryly dismissive of most poetic fashions. While he made Robinson out to be almost wholly tragic, he knew full well what fun the senior poet could be. Of a meeting with Ezra Pound in London in 1913, Frost recalled,

> The first poet we talked about, to the best of my recollection, was Edwin Arlington Robinson. I was fresh from America and

from having read *The Town Down the River.* Beginning at that book, I have slowly spread my reading of Robinson twenty years backward and forward, about equally in both directions.

I remember the pleasure with which Pound and I laughed over the fourth "thought" in

> Miniver thought, and thought, and thought,
> And thought about it.

Three "thoughts" would have been "adequate" as the critical praise-word then was. There would have been nothing to complain of, if it had been left at three. The fourth made the intolerable touch of poetry. With the fourth, the fun began.

Frost appreciated the mischief in Robinson's sorrow, lauded him as a poet of griefs more than grievances, adding that "Robinson could make lyric talk like drama." If this praise also serves to damn, more or less, the long poems on which Robinson spent his later years, it still goes far in explaining what endures in the shorter and medium-length works.

Compare Robinson's poems from the 1890s to others being published at the time, and you will see that he had modernized himself before the Modernists, before Yeats, before practically anybody. From his earliest glimmers of ambition he understood that he wanted his art not to call too much attention to itself, eschewing poetic diction and most archaisms, most syntactical inversions for the sake of a rhyme. Where Whitman and Yeats carry the "egotistical sublime" to the nth degree, Robinson practically disappears into the world of his characters. Even in the marvelous portrait of him painted by Lilla Cabot Perry, Robinson's eyes do not quite meet the viewer's. Tall enough to be nicknamed Long Robinson, ruddy-cheeked, gray-suited, he is the picture of reserve, his right hand loosely fingering the stub of a cigar. Famous for reticence and shyness except when in his cups, Robinson transmuted biographical material into the lives of more than two hundred characters.

And what a biography! There was enough familial suffering for several Eugene O'Neills topped by a goodly helping of Sylvia Plaths, yet Robinson endured his own dark phases as well as those of friends and relatives to make of his life a quiet triumph. As Donaldson has it in his opening sentence, "This book derives from the conviction that Edwin Arlington Robinson was a great American poet and an exceptionally fine human being." The two traits usually cancel each other out, but Robinson as friend and poet proves a model worth emulating, a splendid mix of toughness, humor and compassion. When one young writer at the MacDowell Colony was seen to throw himself prostrate on the ground in despair, Robinson quipped, "The ants will get him." But his generosity to friends, and theirs to him, is the stuff of legend.

Donaldson tells the life deftly, starting with the poet's birth in Head Tide, Maine, the third son of Edward, a successful businessman, and Mary, a would-be poet. The family soon moved to Gardiner, a town Amy Lowell would call "so English in its atmosphere." Edwin Arlington Robinson's name was a burden to him, but family shortened it to Win and friends eventually used initials, calling him EAR—rather ironic since he was deaf in his right ear after being whacked by a teacher for daydreaming in class.

At first it appeared that his older brothers, Herman and Dean, would be the family success stories. Herman went into banking, speculating in land as far away as St. Louis and the Twin Cities, while Dean became a promising doctor. Unfortunately, at about the time Win was drifting toward Harvard, where he would spent two years as a "special student," everything began to crumble for the Robinsons. His father's health declined, and he died in 1892, after Win's first year of college. Herman stole and married Emma Shepherd, with whom Win had been deeply but clumsily in love, and Dean became addicted to morphine.

As it turned out Herman was not a world-class businessman. His ventures fizzled soon after he married Emma, and he embarked on a life of pipedreams and alcoholic decline. By the time Win returned from Harvard in 1893 he was the only stable male left in the family, a man with no practical ambition whatsoever. He worked on their sprawling property, wrote poems, made new friends and stayed in touch with old ones, keeping his literary ambitions largely to himself.

When Mary Robinson died of diphtheria in 1896, EAR was just about to publish his first collection, *The Torrent and the Night Before,* having paid fifty-two dollars printing costs. Contrary to myth, the book was widely praised despite the words "PRINTED

FOR THE AUTHOR" on its title page, yet it did not lead to a contract with a commercial house. Still, the fact that it included early masterpieces like "George Crabbe," "Luke Havergal," "The House on the Hill" and "The Clerks" has led several recent critics to see it as a landmark volume. A year later, again self-published, came *The Children of the Night*, a revised and expanded version of the first book. Again reviewers paid attention, but editors largely did not. Robinson made seventeen dollars on sales and had no further prospects. College friends and others did what they could to support him. One of these, Willie Butler, even sold Robinson's books in his Boston department store.

After a final blowup with Herman over Emma, Robinson left Gardiner, more or less for good. His first job was as assistant to Charles Eliot Norton, the great president of Harvard, but regular employment never agreed with Robinson, and he quit after a year. The deafness in one ear, his usual shyness and stubborn adherence to the life of poetry hardly made him an ideal employee. He had avoided marriage, becoming instead a beloved uncle to his nieces, and his family was a wreck. Dean had died of a morphine overdose in 1899; Herman's alcoholism was rapidly making him unemployable, an impossible husband and father.

It would take Robinson a decade to write the remarkable poem alluding to Dean's death. Notice that "How Annandale Went Out" takes place between quotation marks, the understated account of a doctor who apparently approves of euthanasia:

> "They called it Annandale—and I was there
> To flourish, to find words, and to attend:
> Liar, physician, hypocrite, and friend,
> I watched him; and the sight was not so fair
> As one or two that I have seen elsewhere:
> An apparatus not for me to mend—
> A wreck, with hell between him and the end,
> Remained of Annandale; and I was there.
>
> "I knew the ruin as I knew the man;
> So put the two together if you can,
> Remembering the worst you know of me.
> Now view yourself as I was, on the spot—
> With a slight kind of engine. Do you see?
> Like this . . . You wouldn't hang me? I thought not."

The full measure of Robinson's anguish concerning his brothers lay in his silence about them except in a few poems. Some of his closest friends did not know about Dean. Others knew there was a woman in Robinson's past, but little more. The poems would demonstrate broad sympathy for people of all walks of life, including several about prostitutes (Donaldson is appropriately cautious about the poet's minimal sex life). Robinson may be one of the least judgmental poets we have, as far from self-aggrandizement as one can get this side of the monastery. He accepted loans when they came, sometimes managed to pay them back, and felt that he owed at least poems and copies of his manuscripts to those who helped.

It is instructive to be reminded of Robinson's years of poverty in New York, his work as a subway time keeper and his increasing dependence upon alcohol to numb himself against many kinds of personal pain. He seems to have done without sex rather more than many of us could, relying upon friendships with both men and women to keep up his spirits. When one of his friends fell in love (like Robinson) with his brother's wife, EAR wrote him a long, thoughtful letter, which Donaldson quotes in full. Perhaps the most telling passage is this:

What I am most afraid of in your case is that you are in danger of forgetting that even the most hellish of human complexities are not to be considered too bitterly in the beginning. We cannot measure anything until we have seen it through.

What is it but wisdom, or enough of wisdom to make endurance possible? That, friendship, the occasional loan and a generous sense of humor saw Robinson through many hard times, including the eventual suicide of his old friend Willie Butler—an act with an eerie resemblance to Richard Cory's in EAR's most anthologized poem.

The neglect of editors is particularly galling in this story. When Robinson finally secured a commercial contract to publish a new book, *Captain Craig,* one of the publisher's staff "paid a visit to a Boston brothel, left the manuscript behind, and quite forgot about it." Luckily, the obliging madam recognized the value of the book and returned it. Unluckily, the book did not do very well when published in 1902. One of its few champions was the Harvard classicist Trumbull Stickney, who was to die of a brain tumor just two years later. Robinson was becoming the Job of poets.

The great story of his rescue from poverty by none other than Theodore Roosevelt has never been better told than in Donaldson's book. Kermit Roosevelt, the president's youngest son, was a student at the Groton School, where he heard a teacher reading Robinson's poems aloud and was entranced. Kermit would also become an alcoholic and depressive, committing suicide in 1943, but as a boy he shared his father's ebullience. He bought two copies of *The Children of the Night*, presenting them to his parents as gifts in 1904. Teddy, too, was taken by the poems and alarmed to learn of the poet's plight. After several attempts to help, he eventually convinced EAR to accept a sinecure in the Custom House in lower Manhattan. Teddy even reviewed Robinson's poems for two papers, causing the poet more than a little embarrassment among his literary connections. But think of it—a sitting U.S. president saving a poet! It's one of the most heartening tales in the history of American letters.

Robinson's duties in the Custom House were minimal: he should show up, read the newspaper and leave it folded on his chair before going home to write poems. Without the usual adversity coming between him and his work, he felt nearly paralyzed, producing little new work. But the election of William Howard Taft in 1908 put an end to the sinecure. Robinson soon plunged into poverty again, desperate to save himself through success as a novelist or playwright. It never happened. Even in his late, lucrative verse novels on Arthurian subjects, Robinson lacked one gift necessary to the longer work—a sense of what propels a story over time, what makes a reader anxious to turn the pages. It might be that he lacked the requisite vulgarity to give life to the longer form, and was far better working on short or medium-length poems.

In 1910 he published *The Town Down the River*, another strong collection containing poems like "Miniver Cheevy," "Two Gardens of Linndale," "Calverly's" and "Uncle Ananias," a charming portrait of a liar. His poem on Lincoln, "The Master," was typically critical of those who judge too quickly:

> A flying word from here and there
> Had sown the name at which we sneered,
> But soon the name was everywhere,
> To be reviled and then revered:
> A presence to be loved and feared,
> We cannot hide it, or deny
> That we, the gentlemen who jeered,
> May be forgotten by and by.

This is more schematic than Robinson's best, but as a meditation on fame and the follies of criticism it still carries weight.

From 1911 onward Robinson's life fell into a basic pattern. The newly established MacDowell Colony would take him in annually from summer through much of the fall, after which he would reside in Spartan simplicity in New York or Boston. At MacDowell he was generally sober and industrious, taking up serious drinking again only in 1919 to protest Prohibition. His *Collected Poems* of 1922 won the first of three Pulitzer Prizes, and he began to make real money as a poet. The first of his Arthurian epics, *Tristan*, was a Literary Guild selection, selling seventy-two thousand copies in a year. The mendicant in Robinson could not resist giving much of his income away, either to repay debts or to help indigent friends. He lived for poetry, scorned literary competition (though he played mean games of poker and pool), hardly ever stepped off his worn path between MacDowell and the city—an extended trip to England being the one exception—and took his new-found eminence, the sales and honorary degrees, with equanimity.

Placing Robinson in the context of modern poetry is only difficult for those who assume that the confessional free verse lyric or self-reflexive language have become the norm. In the greater scheme of things, he remains part of the enduring lyric and narrative traditions that have never gone away, whatever literary propagandists say. When I consider Modernism's formal explosions, I find it almost comical to imagine the author of "Richard Cory" attending the Armory Show in February 1913:

The exhibition introduced the work of Matisse, Picasso, Cezanne, Van Gogh, and others to the American public. The most controversial painting was Marcel Duchamp's abstract "Nude Descending a Staircase," which reminded Theodore Roosevelt of a Navajo blanket. Robinson had a somewhat similar reaction. Although he professed to approve of experimentation in art as well as in science, his own tastes did not incline to the avant garde. "I went to . . . the big Art Show the other evening," he wrote to [Hermann] Hagedorn, "and since then I've been trying to decide who's crazy."

Proponents of literary revolution usually come around to a belief in enduring verities. The lesser poems of Robinson are those sounding stiff-limbed to our ears today, like creaking Edwardians. Yet some of his poems in what amount to "old-fashioned measures"—"Luke Havergal" or "Eros Turannos," for example— possess an uncanny dramatic quality that gets under the skin.

Teddy Roosevelt had proclaimed his admiration for "Luke Havergal" while confessing that he did not understand it, but then Teddy was a better reader than some of our literary critics. As Eliot would later say, one has to be able to derive pleasure from poetry before the critical faculty kicks in with its machinery of explanation. Robinson's best poems invite this sort of reading because he usually leaves important matters unstated. We can say "Luke Havergal" is about temptation to suicide, but such paraphrase misses the incantatory hauntings of the verse:

> There is the western gate, Luke Havergal,
> There are the crimson leaves upon the wall.
> Go, for the winds are tearing them away,—
> Nor think to riddle the dead words they say,
> Nor any more to feel them as they fall;
> But go, and if you trust her she will call.
> There is the western gate, Luke Havergal—
> Luke Havergal.

Confronted with such rhythms and insistent rhymes, most editors in our time would snort derisively and reach for the circular file. In a sense, we have been spoiled by our tin-eared mythologies of innovation. It takes the sort of literary devotion I mentioned earlier to read "Luke Havergal" with enjoyment, a willingness to read outside the limits of current fashion. The renewed energies brought to bear by Modernism met Robinson's approval, though he was not able to write free verse himself. "I write badly enough as it is," he joked. By the same token, Harriet Monroe, founder of *Poetry*, recognized a contemporary in Robinson. Receiving "Eros Turannos" in the mail, "she wrote 'Jewel' at the top of the page" and published it in the March 1914 issue.

A year later, the June 1915 issue of *Poetry* would include Eliot's "The Love Song of J. Alfred Prufrock" as well as Pound's review of Frost. The simultaneity of these multiple strands of modern poetry is difficult to grasp, but like Frost's brilliant "Home Burial," Robinson's "Eros Turannos" is a chillingly modern portrait of an unequal marriage, as realistic psychologically as anything in Eliot:

> She fears him, and will always ask
> What fated her to choose him;
> She meets in his engaging mask
> All reasons to refuse him;
> But what she meets and what she fears
> Are less than are the downward years,
> Drawn slowly to the foamless weirs
> Of age were she to lose him.

It's a dramatic sound matching the best of Kipling and Hardy.

He could also be darkly comic. One of the perennial favorites among his later poems is "Mr. Flood's Party"—certainly, along with Li Bai's "Drinking Alone with the Moon," among the most affecting things I have read about drunkenness. Notice the painstaking balance of line and rhetoric—for example, the delayed verb of the opening sentence:

> Old Eben Flood, climbing alone one night
> Over the hill, between the town below
> And the forsaken upland hermitage
> That held as much as he should ever know
> On earth again of home, paused warily.

What ensues is a drunken man's dialogue with himself, a to-and-fro suitable for a punning name like Eben Flood. Robinson's own brother Herman became a lush like this, dying horribly of tuberculosis at forty-four, but though Eben is another of the poet's ruined, isolated romantics, the poem never succumbs to bathos. W. C. Fields might have had fun with it:

> Then, as a mother lays her sleeping child
> Down tenderly, fearing it may awake,
> He set the jug down slowly at his feet
> With trembling care, knowing that most things break;
> And only when assured that on the earth
> It stood, as the uncertain lives of men
> Assuredly did not, he paced away,
> And with his hand extended, paused again:
>
> "Well, Mr. Flood, we have not met like this
> In a long time; and many a change has come
> To both of us, I fear, since last it was
> We had a drop together. Welcome home!"
> Convivially returning to himself,
> Again he raised the jug up to the light;
> And with an acquiescent quaver said:
> "Well, Mr. Flood, if you insist, I might."

The drunk is delusional; Robinson is not. His skepticism about human knowledge makes him, like the ancient Greeks, perennially modern. In one early letter to a critic he had written, "The world is not a 'prison-house' but a kind of spiritual kindergarten, where millions of bewildered infants are trying to spell God with the wrong blocks." He knew enough to turn the same insight everywhere. "I should not rush to see myself too well," he wrote in *Amaranth* (1934), one of his more highly regarded longer poems, "Or to behold myself too finally, / If I were you."

Donaldson's account of the poet's last years is frankly moving. At the end, doctors kept the truth of his pancreatic cancer from him, and he labored away at the proofs of *King Jasper* from his hospital bed. At one point he slipped into a coma, but emerged just long enough to finish the work.

I once heard Stephen Spender say of W. H. Auden that he had never known anyone with so focused a life. Auden identified his ambition early, achieved it, and promptly died at age sixty-six. Robinson's life took a very different path, more crooked, less influential on a global scale, but he was just as singularly devoted. We are heirs to his devotion—as well as a few dozen great poems—and we should honor it.

# The Inner Drama of James Wright

James Wright's letters intrigue by a troubled humanity. They hide nothing of his interior conflict between a hope for beauty and terror of disintegration. A new volume of them, *A Wild Perfection: The Selected Letters of James Wright,* also dramatizes a problem in American poetry—the conflict between what had come to seem a stifling academic formalism and the "new poetry" propounded by the school of Bly, the so-called Deep Image poets of the 1960s. Wright was tugged between these poles, often declaring that his two favorite poets were Edwin Arlington Robinson and Walt Whitman, the first a formal realist and the second an ecstatic free-verser. Like Bly he was an internationalist, by nature sympathetic to surrealism. He was also a man who resisted his own tendencies toward the romantic and the sentimental, and who loved both hard-bitten realism and traditional meter. He embodied the vital contradictions of American poetry in his day. Perhaps this is partly why he remains an important figure even when we cannot agree how he was (or is) important. As Donald Hall has observed, "It is difficult for people, even today, to love both sides of James Wright—Neruda and Robinson, Trakl and Hardy."

But Wright was loved, and it is fair to say that something of his human story, the drama of these letters, transcends his accomplishments and survives his deficiencies as a poet. In "Lament for a Maker," quoted above, Hall also asks, "Has any American poet been the subject of so many elegies?" And, I would add, from so many different poetic camps? Wright's greatest flaw as a writer— a loss of control over his own impulse to sentimentality—was the very vulnerability that made him so attractive to others. The letters help us understand this by showing us a man more self-aware, more dignified in his struggles, than we might otherwise

have realized. This personal drama, climaxing in a kind of fulfillment, is perhaps best laid out in chronological order.


## Apprenticeship

Born in 1927 the son of working-class parents in Ohio, Wright
early fell in love with poetry as a means of escape. He especially
loved Byron and Keats, and formed an early attachment to Catullus. Through translation from Latin in high school he began
to compose his own poems. Even after enlisting in the army in
1946 he corresponded with high school teachers and friends
about his poetic aspirations. This apprenticeship intensified
during his years at Kenyon College (1948–51), where he studied
with John Crowe Ransom, among others, and forged some of
his longest-lasting literary friendships. He wrote a thesis on
Thomas Hardy, married the Greek American Eleutheria (Liberty) Kardules, then traveled to Vienna on a Fulbright Fellow-
ship, where he translated Theodor Storm and Georg Trakl. At
the University of Washington (1954–56) he began a dissertation
on Dickens, but also studied poetry with Theodore Roethke and
Stanley Kunitz. His friends there included Carolyn Kizer, David
Wagoner and Richard Hugo.

You can already see a scattershot pattern in these friendships
and influences, intense emotionalism combined with sophistication. At age nineteen he wrote a sentence that would haunt
his lifelong practice: "I would rather sacrifice technical skill
than sincerity." He wrote this to a Professor McCreight, friend of
his high school teacher, who sent him the poems of Catullus to
study. But his declaration went against the ascendant New Criticism; he would often be an outsider in hidebound academic
circles. A year later he wrote to another friend, "If my letters
savor of any undue unhappiness, it is surely a reflection of my
reading and of my struggle against the romanticism toward
which I tend. How I long for realism! On the other side of realism, somewhere, lies true Nirvana." The dramatic tension that
would make his best and his worst poetry was already in place.
Throw in his study of poets in other languages, his voracious but
unsystematic reading of fiction, and you begin to understand

his literary character. Then add more volatile elements—incipient alcoholism and depression, massive self-doubts making him vulnerable to other powerful personalities.

Susan Lamb, the friend who received those sentences about realism, also opened a long, remarkable letter in 1949 from a twenty-one-year-old Wright who was thinking ahead to the "architecture" of a life's work in poetry. He was familiar with Japanese literature (having been stationed briefly in Japan), and steeped in the Germans, including Rilke—in short, the sort of obsessive student clearly marked for poetry. He could ramble and pontificate with the worst of us (and, to tell the truth, his occasional self-pity in the letters strains a reader's patience), but he was also capable of promising lyric flights and close observation. He was of two minds about "culture," as he wrote to Robert Mezey from Vienna in 1953:

> But now I am sick of Vienna and Europe. It is too heavy, too slow, too arty. I long for some of that glorious barbarism, that gratifying bleakness and loneliness which is so much of America to me.

While in graduate school in Seattle, he struck up a correspondence with Hall, ranging over such figures as Mezey, Merwin, Anthony and Roger Hecht, Auden vs. Bogan, J. V. Cunningham, Charles Gullans, etc. The letters are friendly, chatty, and full of charming self-deprecation: "I swear to God one of these days I'm going to give up poetry and go directly in for a life of crime." He took a teaching job at the University of Minnesota, and while trying to support his family and complete his dissertation, finished the poems of his first book, *The Green Wall,* selected by Auden for the Yale Series of Younger Poets and published in 1957.

In Minnesota Wright lived the double life of the academic poet who was not involved in the creative writing industry. That is, his growing list of publications as a poet did him little professional good because he'd been hired as a Dickens scholar. Chafing against academic specialization and feeling trapped in the Midwest he had hoped to escape, he began drinking more heavily, and may already have been missing some of his classes. Among his colleagues were legendary boozers Allen Tate and John Berryman, so one imagines "self-help" was not one of the university's strong suits at the time. Wright had soon suffered at least one of the nervous breakdowns that resulted in hospitalization and that become a recurring motif in this book.

Still, he experienced undeniable success. His first book was widely discussed. He was launched as a poet. Re-reading *The Green Wall* at this distance, it seems very Robinsonian, not only in its meters and its narratives, but also in its occasional lack of finesse. A handful of these poems seem fully commanding and accomplished to me now: "A Poem About George Doty in the Death House," "A Song for the Middle of the Night," "A Fit Against the Country" (one line of which gave the book its title), and "Sappho." But it's a book of broad sympathies and real ambition. It made Wright a poet to watch.

### A Crisis of Imagination

Two literary friendships dominate the letters of the next decade—with James Dickey and Robert Bly. This was the decade of Dickey's best work as a poet and critic, and while it may be difficult for us to remember now, he looked hard to beat in the American poetry sweepstakes. Like Wright a fan of Robinson, he displayed both Dionysian violence and Apollonian judgment. He was a vital poet, and Wright's letters to him are richly textured, by turns apologetic and feisty, often musing on the nature of their acquaintance:

> There is a decorum in a growing friendship that I believe in, because genuine friendship, like genuine anything (genuine poetry, for example) is often startling and disturbing—i.e., reviving and restoring to one's spirit; so the decorum is not a dull and trite form, but a necessity.

Their correspondence had begun with a strong disagreement, though Wright's emotional honesty at this point helped them form a close bond.

But it's the letters to Bly which form the real core of this collection. In 1958 Bly sent James Wright a copy of his new magazine, *The Fifties*. This was the year before Wright published his second volume, *Saint Judas,* which remained traditional in form, owing much again to Hardy and Robinson, but was also curiously less dominated by realism than the earlier book, as if he were groping for some ill-defined metaphysics. The encounter with Bly's magazine and its editor's charismatic (at times crackpot) proselytizing against academic poetry posed an immediate challenge to Wright. You can almost witness the chemical reaction when these two men meet on the page. He saw the validity of Bly's attack, but also knew that much of what he loved (including iambic meter) needed to be defended against this onslaught. Only too willing to dismiss his own accomplishments as "displays of all the current cute tricks of meter and rhyme," Wright succumbed to Bly's influence while secretly preserving his affections, which he would confess to more understanding friends like Dickey. Soon after reading Bly's magazine, he wrote to Donald Hall,

> I found myself in a confusion that was not only intellectual—
> it was deeply and emotionally painful to me to discover that
> at the very depth of my consciousness I was divided—really
> divided, as on the blade of a sword—between my loyalty to
> those of my contemporaries who were trying to write with in-
> tellectual grace and to those, far more disturbing and ruth-
> less, who were raising hell and demanding greatness.

If American poetry was becoming a struggle between advocates of the cooked and the raw, Wright felt medium rare.

Of course Bly's rebellion was different from that of the Beats—less involved with Zen and mind-altering substances, less a matter of youthful romanticism, and more a matter of reconceiving genuineness under the influence of other poetries, particularly Hispanic and German. It was not a return to the internationalism of Pound and Eliot, which had confirmed an elite corps of professor-critics, but a championing of popular surrealism, sometimes conveyed through hasty translations. Bly developed a poetics of omission, a paring down of the verbal apparatus of poetry in order to access the psychic liberation he understood in Jungian terms. He loved Yeats as an example, but apparently did so more for the vision than the rigor of his art. This profound suspicion of felicity—the sort of serious playfulness represented by Auden—created an unavoidable alternative tradition, especially in a time of great social upheaval, but Bly's many besotted followers went a bit batty over it, abetted by his Messianic energy. Wright fell under the spell, yet the letters suggest that he compartmentalized his friendships, confessing to some what he dared not repeat to others. With Dickey he discussed Yvor Winters, with Bly Georg Trakl.

The same inner turmoil allowed Wright to offer some rather sensible observations on the art:

> But do I make myself clear about the two necessary steps of creation of great and original poetry? 1. Mastery of formal competence in one's tradition (there is *always* tradition, and it's as ruthlessly inescapable as breathing, hunger, and death. Those who deny the existence of the past, said Santayana in a line which makes me shudder with fear, are doomed endlessly to repeat its mistakes). 2. Then the *breaking through* this formal competence, in order to *create* a poetry which is unique and all one's own: the truly shaped voice of one's self.

Robert and Carol Bly were also important as loyal friends. They lived on a farm in southwestern Minnesota, which became Wright's primary refuge as long as he lived in the area. At times they were joined by poets like Hall and Dickey, Louis Simpson and Thomas McGrath. These must have been boozy, heady visits. When the Sixties Press published *Twenty Poems of César Vallejo,* which he translated with Robert Bly and John Knoepfle, Wright provded a short prose statement indicative of the moment:

> Current poets in the United States seem to be perishing on either side of a grey division between century-old British formalism on the one hand and anti-poetry on the other. In Vallejo we may see a great poet who lives neither in formalism nor in violence, but in imagination.

But the dichotomy presented here is a false one, as Wright must have known, for the imagination thrives in many kinds of poetry. Bly's efforts to liberate consciousness led many poets into puritanical plainness and ultimately impoverished the art. Wright, in short, was wise to resist Bly even as he embraced him.

*Saint Judas* (1959) had contained two of his best poems: the title sonnet and "At the Executed Murderer's Grave." *A Wild Perfection* offers an appendix of poems in draft, including a version of the latter poem as it appeared in *Poetry*. It's a disheartening performance, as clotted and overwrought as the worst of the early Lowell, and turning to the version Wright eventually published in his second book, one can see how profoundly he improved the poem through revision (apparently at Dickey's suggestion). "I croon my tears at fifty cents per line," he writes in the final version, while the one from *Poetry* offers such doozies as this: "But my grammatical cries provide small time, / Small hope for naked victims dropped in lime."

*The Branch Will Not Break* (1963) shows Bly's influence particularly in the move away from iambic meter in such well-known poems as "Autumn Begins in Martins Ferry, Ohio," "Lying in a Hammock at William Duffy's Farm in Pine Island, Minnesota" (with its overreaching, Rilkean ending), "A Blessing" and "Two Hangovers." But some of Wright's strongest writing remains in meter, like the second part of his "Two Poems About President Harding":

> America goes on, goes on
> Laughing, and Harding was a fool.
> Even his big pretentious stone
> Lays him bare to ridicule.
> I know it. But don't look at me.
> By God, I didn't start this mess.
> Whatever moon and rain may be,
> The hearts of men are merciless.

Still a poet of American history and culture, Wright now also tended toward a dissolving self, a sympathy beyond words. But poetry is made of words, and his occasional attempts to transcend his medium can be maddeningly vague, as in "The Jewel":

There is this cave
In the air behind my body
That nobody is going to touch:
A cloister, a silence
Closing around a blossom of fire.
When I stand upright in the wind,
My bones turn to dark emeralds.

Ultimately what I find here and in *Shall We Gather at the River*
(1968) is evidence of a split personality. The Good James Wright
wrote poems of sympathy and precision, while the Bad called up
standard Deep Image tropes—shadows, moon, stone, trees (any
trees would do)—in a vaporous profundity. The Good gave us
"Two Postures Beside a Fire" and "In Response to the Rumor
That the Oldest Whorehouse in Wheeling, West Virginia, Has
Been Condemned." The Bad opened a poem with "Today I am
walking alone in a bare place, / And winter is here." Finally, the
Bad published *Two Citizens* (1973), which Wright quickly realized was his worst book.

The sixties were a decade when Wright nearly succumbed to
his demons. His alcoholism and the catty atmosphere of the
University of Minnesota were not a good mix. Divorced from
Liberty in 1962 and denied tenure, he taught briefly at Moor-
head State, across the Red River from Fargo, North Dakota. He
subsequently taught at Macalester College in Saint Paul, then in
1966 took an appointment at Hunter College in New York,
where he would work for the rest of his life. In 1967 he married
Edith Anne Runk (familiarly known as Annie). He got sober
with the help of Alcoholics Anonymous and, despite occasional
hospitalizations for depression, was generally embarked on his
happiest and most fulfilling years. His *Collected Poems* won the
Pulitzer Prize, and after the misstep of *Two Citizens* he produced
more rigorous and surprising poetry.

The friendship with Bly survived their geographical separation, but Wright tried to outgrow the Deep Image aesthetic. He
had always said he wanted his poems to be those of a "grown
man," and these letters are heartening evidence that a degree of
personal happiness did not get in his way.

## The Grown Man

In 1978 Wright responded to a letter from Roger Jones, who had asked about Deep Image poetry:

> As for my own work, I am almost certain that what some critics have called "deep imagery" and "surrealism" in it is actually just the confusion that results from bad writing. My intention has always been to be as clear as possible. For example, in the poem which you mention, "Written on a Bus in Central Ohio," you say that the poem "seems a very good piece for the conveying of sensory impressions, but is somewhat confusing beyond that." No wonder. There *is* nothing "beyond that."

It's refreshing to find Wright so openly critical of his own failures—utterly undefensive, willing to take responsibility for them. More than once he writes of his appreciation of critical reviews from which he can actually learn through engagement with another mind, rather than hatchet jobs in which the critic's only purpose is to exalt himself: "Some fellow (I've forgotten his name) in *The Hudson Review* sounded as if he were quivering all over like Lionel Barrymore. His review might have given him a hernia."

Another sign of Wright's maturity was his devotion to teaching. He took pride in not being part of the creative writing world, but "a real teacher with a real subject matter." In 1968 he wrote to his own teacher, John Crowe Ransom,

> I can't say that I am concentrating on the book right now. I am rather trying to teach well, for I care about teaching as passionately as I've cared about poetry. You undoubtedly know how I failed as a teacher at the University of Minnesota. True enough, but now I have shown myself to be a good teacher at Hunter.

These letters convince me that Wright was indeed a good teacher at this point in his life. Young people wrote to him and he wrote back, taking them seriously as individuals interested in poetry, but also opening up to them emotionally. This book contains a few of his well-known letters to Leslie Marmon Silko (the bulk of them published in *The Delicacy and Strength of Lace*). There are also wonderful letters to a teenager named Janice Thurn who elicits Wright's warmth and good humor. Furthermore, in the years after his divorce from Liberty, Wright maintained a good, fatherly tone with his sons, Franz and Marshall. When Franz determined to become a poet (like his father a depressive who went on to win a Pulitzer), James Wright was characteristically generous with advice and encouragement.

There are gaps in the letters, to be sure. While a note on the back of this book maintains that Wright corresponded with Dickey until the end of his life, this volume produces no letter to Dickey later than 1965, causing me to wonder if they had a falling-out. And while there are letters to Roger Hecht, we get none to his older brother, Anthony, who would later write an elegy for Wright. Were Anthony Hecht's papers examined for letters? I ask only because Wright would have written differently to Hecht than to Bly, and this difference might have been illuminating.

One of my favorite comic passages in the present selection occurs in a letter written to Richard Hugo from Taranto, Italy, in 1979, Wright's last year. He had been trying to nap in a Naples hotel:

Somebody upstairs was playing a radio loud with rock music. I lay there a while, cursing my fate at being born a contemporary of Bob Dylan, Bruce Springsteen, The Rhythm Method, The Motherfuckers, and Meatloaf, when suddenly I heard something so loud that it required a complete reorientation of my nervous system. Maybe it's the way Vesuvius sounded back in the good old days when the whole top half of the mountain blew off.

It turned out to be a wedding party who were having a reception in the restaurant upstairs. They brought their own orchestra with them, including an electric organ. Dear God, I heard speeches, community renderings of old Neapolitan songs, raucous laughter, and what sounded like Wilt Chamberlain dribbling Truman Capote's head down court for a dunk-shot.

But I did not hear rock music. The Neapolitan wedding party had destroyed it.

The man in these later letters is less inclined to whine and wring his hands, more often moved to love the world, as if anticipating his early departure from it. I still find his poetry a mixed bag, but the mixture is perhaps more assured and less mannered. Starting with *To a Blossoming Pear Tree* (1977) and continuing in the final poems of *This Journey* (1982), Wright alternated prose vignettes with his verses. The letters tell us that he did not believe in the prose poem (a term he called "idiotically confused"), but among aficionados of the form Wright is considered a master. Poems like "With the Shell of a Hermit Crab" and "Lighting a Candle for W. H. Auden" demonstrate his continued facility with rhyme and meter, while "The Best Days," "Hook" and "To a Blossoming Pear Tree" offer free verse realism and sympathy for beings other than himself. *This Journey* begins with a free verse poem, followed by a rhymed one, followed by prose, as if to announce that, whatever else you can say about James Wright, he was never reduced by the "poetry wars." I rather like the prose bits called "Against Surrealism," "In Memory of the Ottomans" and "Honey," as well as his truncated ballade, "Between Wars."

At his best, Wright balanced his sympathy with more determined artistry, lucidity with an openness to what cannot be fully understood. The letters give us a sometimes painful evolution, arriving at a maturity visible in his strongest late poems. Here, as a closing example, is the final stanza of "The Journey":

> Many men
> Have searched all over Tuscany and never found
> What I found there, the heart of the light
> Itself shelled and leaved, balancing
> On filaments themselves falling. The secret
> Of this journey is to let the wind
> Blow its dust all over your body.
> To let it go on blowing, to step lightly, lightly
> All the way through your ruins, and not to lose
> Any sleep over the dead, who surely
> Will bury their own, don't worry.

# "The Contemplation of Horror Is Not Edifying"

## Anthony Hecht as a War Poet

One day in the middle 1980s I found myself sitting in a faculty lounge with Anthony Hecht, a poet I admired to distraction. I was a graduate student in my early thirties, Hecht an eminence about to leave the University of Rochester for an appointment at Georgetown, where he would later by special arrangement co-direct my dissertation on Auden. I had worked in Alaska, lived in Greece, failed at most literary and personal ambitions while laboring as a gardener, but that day Hecht paid me an unexpected compliment. Not given to effusive emotions with people he barely knew, he told me I reminded him of men he had known on the G.I. Bill after the war. My eager pursuit of literary knowledge could not be divorced from a broader experience of struggle in life.

I had almost forgotten that afternoon until, sitting down to write this essay on Hecht as a war poet, I realized he was also touching on aspects of himself. This most elaborate, even baroque, of modern poets would not have been the writer he was without painful knowledge of what lay outside the intellectual life, especially his horrific journey across Europe as a soldier in the Ninety-seventh Infantry Division. For Tony, as I came to call him, the compensations of art and learning were partly a refuge from horror, partly an illumination of it. His realism—present even in poems where he deliberately pushed artifice to extremes—resulted from his witness to and participation in a major global catastrophe.

My own "worldliness" could not really be compared to his. In Alaska I had bunked on an old troop ship, and in a smaller vessel sailed from Dutch Harbor to Kodiak Island during a stomach-churning storm. I had seen extremes of human behavior and some violence, but nothing like the mechanized slaughter Tony witnessed in the war. Despite our very different backgrounds, though—my West Coast origins, his New York upbringing—we understood the formalities of art to exist for more than themselves. Life without the shaping impulse can be hard for some of us to bear.

Calling Hecht a war poet may not appear to acknowledge all the other subjects he wrote about: art, love, family, madness and disease, birth and death. But his poems dealing directly with the war and the Holocaust are among the very best by any modern poet, and the war with its schooling in irony underlies his poems on other subjects. The happiness of his second marriage, for example, produced poems like "Peripeteia," where beauty is very nearly salvation. Set in a theater before and during a production of Shakespeare's *The Tempest*, the poem becomes a dream of art and redemption. The unmentioned war is present, I would argue, as part of the reality he would like to be saved from, including the cynical intrigue forming the background to Shakespeare's play: "Something is happening. Some consternation. / Are the knives out? Is someone's life in danger? / And can the magic cloak and book protect?" It is implicit knowledge propelling the pilgrim poet on his journey toward the sublime.

By the same token, the ornate, painterly detail of "The Venetian Vespers" arises from a sensitive mind in the process of breaking down. The narrator is a veteran who recalls "a corporal I knew in Heavy Weapons, / Someone who carried with him into combat / A book of etiquette by Emily Post." This absurd juxtaposition of manners and warfare characterizes a technique learned from Auden in which scenes of horror are cast into relief, framed, as it were, by other scenes. Auden's "The Shield of Achilles" sets dark images of impersonal modern warfare against Homeric art, which cannot salve our consciousness of the worst human beings can do. Hecht's "More Light! More Light!" prefaces its brutal Holocaust narrative with another historical scene, the execution by burning of an English martyr, and presents a further irony by using Goethe's last words in its title. "Still Life" would seem to be all pastoral description until the ending reveals the author himself "somewhere in Germany, / A cold, wet, Garand rifle in my hands." And "The Book of Yolek," another masterpiece about the Holocaust, sets the starvation of children in the camps against the prosperity of American homes where we might enjoy a "meal / Of grilled brook trout." These poems by Auden and Hecht are among the most moving in modern English, but they succeed by virtue of their deeply ironic doubleness and cold intelligence, their dramatic structures as well as their calculated use of high and low diction, moments of beauty and moments of brutal frankness.

In "The Venetian Vespers" no book of etiquette can save that remembered soldier:

> He haunts me here, that seeker after law
> In a lawless world, in rainsoaked combat boots,
> Oil-stained fatigues and heavy bandoleers.
> He was killed by enemy machine-gun fire.
> His helmet had fallen off. They had sheered away
> The top of his cranium like a soft-boiled egg,
> And there he crouched, huddled over his weapon,
> His brains wet in the chalice of his skull.

Dramatic details laden with irony are used to withering effect—those "brains wet in the chalice of his skull," the word "chalice" coming out of another world. Like Yeats, and before him Keats, Hecht's narrator desires an escape "From time, from history, from evolution / Into the blessed stasis of a painting. . . ." For Keats the escape never quite happens. He is forever falling back into mortality. And though Yeats declares that he will take the form of a golden bird in "Sailing to Byzantium," even then the escape from reality is incomplete. The bird will sing "Of what is past, or passing, or to come," the world in which we live, change, and die. When Hecht's narrator says of his beautiful vision "I look and look, / As though I could be saved simply by looking," he acknowledges salvation is not quite achieved. Necessity and freedom, reality and imagination, are bound together in symbiosis, each feeding off the other.

Hecht's earliest substantial publications came directly out of the war. A student at Kenyon College on the G. I. Bill, he got to know John Crowe Ransom and submitted his poems to the

*Kenyon Review.* One of the earliest published, "To a Soldier Killed in Germany," could well be a rehearsal for that machine-gun death in "The Venetian Vespers":

> What wonder hit you, turned you inside out,
> Shaking all wonders from you at one blow?
> You could not doubt it was an honest ghost
> Because it killed all doubts, gave you that most
> Terrible killing wound. You could not know
> Doubt is the wound we cannot do without.

The poem was never reprinted. Surely Hecht came to disapprove of certain labored aspects, from the fruitless allusion to *Hamlet* to the strained philosophizing.

A far more intriguing poem in the same issue (Spring 1947) is "Once Removed," which I shall quote in full:

I saw a piece of hard-earned earth, a piece of the world
Where the wind fell down on rocks, and a hundred sticks
Were all the forest it had, and the water curled
In a dark ring, in a hole.

The air was convulsed, the water split its face on the stones,
And the bitter weather rounded about my soul;
And nothing at all was there to interpret the groans
Or the palsy of the trees.

And seeing this broken landscape tied by the wind together,
I wanted to drop down on my paper knees,
And become some wind-bitten plant, and bend in the
    weather,
And I wanted to scream.

But I thought, "you could not measure the wind's
    magnificent stature,
Being a twig, and tormented as if by a dream,
Or a giant rock, permitting the season to fracture
Your crude, inarticulate face."

So I wandered away from that place where the quaking trees
    called out
And the wind fell down, I wandered away from that place
To find the difficult, dry words about
A forest of a hundred sticks.

Aside from some strain in the fourth stanza, this poem works well, its nearly allegorical battlefield abstracted like the set of a Beckett play. The poet requires "difficult, dry words" to evoke a shattered forest and water-filled foxhole and the groans of the wounded, yet the war is never directly mentioned. As in Hecht's later and far greater poem, "A Hill," which opens *The Hard Hours,* we cannot entirely know what haunts this scene. It is a kind of nightmare, some version of which is present in every book he published.

In his preface to *Poets of World War II* (Library of America, 2003), Harvey Shapiro noticed a lack of piety and patriotism in the American poetry he was collecting. No poet would better represent this observation than Hecht, yet the anthology mistakenly uses too little of his work. His poems are among the most devastating and ironic to come out of that conflict. Irony for Hecht was less a literary device than a sane response to an insane world. He always had contempt for leaders who went blithely into war. Philip Hoy's great interview with Hecht (Between the Lines, 1999) contains several illuminating anecdotes on that score:

> My company had been pinned down by very heavy enemy fire in Germany. Our company commander was a fool, wholly incapable of any initiative, who slavishly obeyed commands, however uninformed or ill-considered, from battalion or regimental HQ, and without regard to the safety or capacity of his troops. (He was later awarded a Silver Star for action that took place on a day when he was behind the lines being treated for dysentery.) Anyway, on this day when we were hopelessly kept flat on the ground by superior fire-power, some idiot at an upper echelon, far behind the lines and blissfully unaware of our situation regarding the enemy . . . , ordered my company to move forward, and the captain ordered us to ready ourselves, though there would have been nothing but total annihilation in prospect. At the last second, higher command called for artillery, which turned the trick. And as we slowly rose from prone positions, I confessed to my platoon commander, a second lieutenant just about my age, that if the order to advance had not been countermanded I was very unsure whether I would have obeyed. "Of course you would have," he replied, but with a look that meant a great deal. He

fully understood how foolish such a command would have been at the time, but as an officer, whose duty was to set an example, he knew that he would have had to obey.

Slightly later Hecht tells of American soldiers mowing down a group of German women and children who were trying to surrender, adding. "that morning left me without the least vestige of patriotism or national pride. And when I hear empty talk about that war having been a 'good war,' as contrasted with, say, Vietnam, I maintain a fixed silence."

In such a context, poetry is at pains to present the truth too often evaded by our politicians. I remember very well Tony's outrage at the invasion of Iraq in 2003, and his anger at the bombing of North Vietnam can be seen in a poem like "An Overview," detailing "the engaging roguishness / With which a youthful bombardier / Unloads his eggs on what appear / The perfect patchwork squares of chess. . . ."

There is a just and purifying anger in such poems, but where the Holocaust was concerned Hecht also experienced nightmares and prolonged despair. He participated in the liberation of Flossenbürg, "an annex of Buchenwald," just after the execution there of Dietrich Bonhoeffer. "Prisoners were dying at the rate of 500 a day from typhus," he told Hoy. "The place, the suffering, the prisoners' accounts were beyond comprehension. For years after I would wake shrieking. I must add an important point: after the war I read widely in Holocaust literature, and I can no longer separate my anger and revulsion at what I really saw from what I later came to learn."

Hecht published his first book, *A Summoning of Stones,* in 1954, but except for a few poems he used his art here to keep the war at bay. Exceptions to this were "Japan," a poem owing its origins to Hecht's post-war service in that country, "Christmas Is Coming," and his "Drinking Song":

> We are indeed diminished.
> We are twelve.
> But have recaptured a sufficiency
> Of France's cognac; and it shall be well,
> Given sufficient time, if we can down

Half of it, being as we are, reduced.
Five dead in the pasture, yet they loom
As thirstily as ever. Are recalled
By daring wagers to this living room:
"I'll be around to leak over your grave."

That last line, evoking both pissing and bleeding, is a particularly Hechtian touch.

His Pulitzer Prize–winning collection, *The Hard Hours* (1967), was rather more unsparing in its acknowledgment of horror. The Eliot-influenced sequence "Rites and Ceremonies" struggles to comprehend unspeakable acts in the context of religious tradition. A section entitled "The Fire Sermon" (with an irony Eliot could not have imagined when he wrote "The Waste Land") ends with verses modeled on George Herbert's "Denial." In Herbert's poem each five-line stanza ends with a line that does not rhyme. The concluding stanza, though, does rhyme, formally suggesting the barest hint of a connection between man and God. Hecht, of course, withholds the rhyme even there, because understanding cannot be achieved in the face of such massive killing. "The contemplation of horror is not edifying," begins a third section, "The Dream." Hecht appears to have accepted that his muse, like Baudelaire's, was a sick one, unable to turn away from what he had seen.

The collection's title comes from a poem addressing one of his sons, "Adam," and the boys from his first marriage appear again in "It Out-Herods Herod. Pray You, Avoid It." They are watching a Western on TV, rapt by a world where "The Good casts out the Bad." The poet, making himself a drink, knows otherwise:

And that their sleep be sound
I say this childermas
Who could not, at one time,
Have saved them from the gas.

As at the end of his later poem "The Book of Yolek," no comfort can protect us from a vision of the dead, no complacency is tenable. The refuge of art and study has its purposes, but salvation and freedom from guilt are not among them.

There is more to say about Anthony Hecht as a war poet, particularly about his deep reading in history, which fueled the irony of his writing. His familiarity with Roman history is evident, for example, in a remarkable poem about trauma and the attempt to be healed, "Behold the Lilies of the Field." One might argue that this reading meshed with his personal experience to produce a dark assessment of human beings. But Hecht could be generous as well. In his best collection of essays, *Melodies Unheard* (2003), it is striking how much sympathy he feels for poets like Seamus Heaney, Yehuda Amichai and Charles Simic, whose only commonality is an experience of war. Such very different writers, like Hecht himself, pursued their art in the face of brutality and were touched by it indelibly.

But Hecht remains more, much more, than a poet of war and death. Any true appraisal of his work will have to take into account his mordant humor, and how, in the last decade of his life, images of joy and fulfillment appeared with greater frequency. Like Yeats, Hecht grew as a man and poet right to the very end. More than Yeats, he delighted in friends and family, loyally supported a host of poets, many of them vastly different from himself. He enjoyed his most productive years in retirement, producing more poems, essays, reviews and introductions. The world did not become less absurd, our leaders less deserving of his wrath, but he had found compensations in love and art that were, after all, very much worth having.

# Mastered Pain

Anthony Hecht was one of the best poets our nation has ever produced, a writer of such ambition and high achievement that it is a shame he is not more widely celebrated. To most readers of poetry he is remembered as the Pulitzer Prize–winning author of a few dark, frequently anthologized poems like "A Hill" and "More Light! More Light!" Or perhaps lighter fare like "The Dover Bitch," a poem that offers alternative points of view from Matthew Arnold's "Dover Beach." But Hecht was more, much more than our resident misanthrope, our nightmare elaborator. He was one of the great synthesizers of modern experience, a visionary poet capable of conveying private experience in public forms—difficult, to be sure, allusive and self-consciously literary in style, but well worth the effort it takes to read him.

*Collected Later Poems,* comprising the complete texts of three later volumes of verse, extends and illuminates the better-known early work. With his last gathering of essays, *Melodies Unheard,* the late work allows us to see a poet unlike anyone else, more extreme than most in his brutal complexities, his active dialogue between reality and art, yet devoid of the egotism marring poetry like Robert Lowell's. When we speak of Lowell, admiring the shocking freshness of his best work, we acknowledge his unevenness as a poet—a charge that cannot be leveled against Hecht. His verse has the high finish of Renaissance sculpture, yet is alive to multiple points of view, multiple social classes and levels of diction. The style is absorbent and technically seamless, even when indulging a penchant for puns and "low" humor.

Hecht mixed rare opulence with an uncompromising and complex moral vision, giving us moments of such gravity that his leavenings of humor and sheer beauty seem all the more memorable. Though he was among the most self-consciously artificial of all our stylists, it's Hecht's disillusionment I most recall. At a time when poets are too happy to clown for coppers from any crowd that will so much as notice them, Hecht remains defiantly difficult, offering penetrating pleasures of the sort one might derive from the novels of Henry James, the essays of John Ruskin, the paintings of Tiepolo. His poems reward attention and re-reading as few contemporary works can even dream of doing.

Anthony Hecht grew up in New York City, son of a businessman whose fortunes rose and fell so precipitously that family life was constantly imploding. Hints of these early years can be found in poems like "Green: An Epistle" and "Apprehensions," both available in *Collected Earlier Poems* (1990). In the interview with Philip Hoy he reported his family's mixture of pride and shame at their Jewish heritage, his brother Roger's epilepsy and other ailments, and a general state of unhappiness throughout childhood. He attended good schools and had several years at Bard College before being drafted at twenty (his bachelor's degree would be awarded *in absentia*). Overseas with the Ninety-seventh Infantry Division, Hecht saw combat in France, Germany and Czechoslovakia, participating in the liberation of a concentration camp at Flossenburg, where Dietrich Bonhoeffer had been murdered just days earlier: "The place, the suffering, the prisoners' accounts were beyond comprehension. For years after I would wake shrieking." Always inclined to seek aesthetic compensations for the pains of reality, he would find in this experience and in decades of later reflection the blunt truth underlying all of his poems: life is so cruel, our sanity so tenuous, that any help offered by art and love is to be cherished beyond measure.

Among the events that set him on his melancholic course was the failure of his first marriage. After a separation in 1959 (the divorce came in 1961) Hecht's wife left with their two young sons, and he fell into a depression requiring hospitalization and a course of Thorazine. Many of Hecht's friends, including Lowell and Anne Sexton, had intimate experience of madness. Yet it must be said that Hecht retained a survivor's instinct those poets lacked, or perhaps was luckier in his brain chemistry. Though he would never have predicted this for himself, his life became a movement toward health and a greater equilibrium than the mad mid-century poets enjoyed. Hecht's immense sadness at the divorce can be felt in poems like "A Letter" and "Adam":

> Adam, there will be
> Many hard hours,
> As an old poem says,
> Hours of loneliness.
> I cannot ease them for you;
> They are our common lot.

But Hecht never whines, never swoons with self-pity, as the so-called confessional poets were wont to do. There is iron in his blood and a persistent rigor in his thought. The story of Hecht's life as a man and poet is of the consistent dignity and mastery of his work, the happiness of his second marriage, the honors heaped on his head, the gradual waning of temperamental mood-swings and the solidifying of poetic command. This happened, of course, in a literary climate that generally lacked the patience to understand a writer of complexity.

He had a stable academic career, teaching for many years at the University of Rochester and finishing at Georgetown. He won most of the honors it is possible for a poet to win this side of the Nobel—which he likely would have been denied simply because he hadn't a populist bone in his body. True, he remained as death-obsessed and generally cynical as ever, but one can also glimpse in the poems the man remembered by his oldest friends for a rollicking sense of humor, the fellow who used to recite swatches of Milton's "Lycidas" in a W. C. Fields accent. Accounting for Hecht means accounting for an artist who has never been easy to measure.

Hecht published seven separate volumes of verse, beginning with *A Summoning of Stones* in 1954, a book of sometimes ornamental poems that was respectfully reviewed and went quickly out of print. More than a dozen difficult and formative years passed before he published *The Hard Hours* (1967), which generally displayed a tougher style and brought Hecht his only Pulitzer. This was followed a decade later by *Millions of Strange*

*Shadows,* another flawless collection, then with relative speed *The Venetian Vespers* (1979). Those three volumes (*The Hard Hours* contains some poems preserved from *A Summoning of Stones*), taking Hecht up to age fifty-six, are enough to assure his place in American literature. They demonstrate his range over many types of poems as well as diverse subjects, and are utterly commanding in their accomplishment. They comprise the *Collected Earlier Poems* published in 1990.

That same year Hecht published *The Transparent Man*, which was followed by *Flight Among the Tombs* (1996) and *The Darkness and the Light* (2001). At this point one might well ask, shouldn't a misanthrope of Hecht's stature have taken a bridge or an overdose by now? Clearly, something more than bile was keeping him alive. While I would hardly describe the *Collected Later Poems* as a joyful book (though it is full of pleasures), it does contain several poems suggesting that Hecht can be surprised by joy as well as rancor. Indeed, Hecht should be numbered among the ranks of poets like Yeats who remain productive into their later years, maintaining a lofty mental agility.

One can't understand Hecht's endurance and vitality without going back to the war. It provided one of the curious meeting places of physical and intellectual experience for him, and in a later essay on "St. Paul's Epistle to the Galatians" (collected in *Melodies Unheard*) he would write:

> As a Jew living in a society essentially secular but nominally Christian, I have felt a need to learn the ways and something of the faith of the majority, for a Gentile is no longer, as in the Hebrew liturgy, "the stranger dwelling in our midst." It is impossible to be a Jew of my generation without being keenly aware of anti-Semitism, and sensitivity on this point alone has invited a study of Christian doctrine.

Compensatory and to some degree self-protective, Hecht's erudition, including deep familiarity with the Bible, is part of the whole fabric of his poetry. Among other literary influences one can easily identify Horace, Shakespeare, Milton, Baudelaire, Eliot, Auden and others, not to mention John Crowe Ransom, his post-war teacher when he was a "special student" on the G.I.

Bill at Kenyon College. The resulting style can be elevated, to put it mildly, but as Hecht noted in the interview with Philip Hoy, "any flamboyance is likely to be confronted or opposed by counter-force, directness, elemental grit."

The most obvious manifestation of this doubleness is in Hecht's technique of juxtaposition. His much-anthologized Holocaust poem "More Light! More Light!" begins with a scene of a long-ago execution—three gruesome stanzas about a man being burnt at the stake. Then the poet makes a simple transition to World War II:

> We move now to outside a German wood.
> Three men are there commanded to dig a hole
> In which the two Jews are ordered to lie down
> And be buried alive by the third, who is a Pole.

Still another historical moment comes by allusion in the poem's title, Goethe's reported last words. The inquisitorial flames of the opening, not assuaged by "prayers in the name of Christ," and the matter-of-fact brutality of a Nazi execution are given uncanny power by the repetition of that word, "light":

> No light, no light in the blue Polish eye.
> When he finished a riding boot packed down the earth.
> The Lüger hovered lightly in its glove.
> He was shot in the belly and in three hours bled to death.

Other poets have given us feasts of gratuitous horror from conflicts of one sort or another, but Hecht's tonal control lifts these lines to the sort of monumental power Auden achieved in his great poem "The Shield of Achilles," which also works by juxtaposing separate moments in time. In Hecht's *Collected Earlier Poems* a number of lyrics and meditative sequences arose from direct experience of war and the Holocaust, or later reading on these events. "The contemplation of horror is not edifying," Hecht avowed in "Rites and Ceremonies," adding, "Neither does it strengthen the soul." It is, however, not to be wished away. Though I find fewer war-related works in *Collected Later Poems,* the book contains at least one more that rises to a level of greatness through this technique of juxtaposition. This is a sestina, "The Book of Yolek," first collected in *The Transparent Man* (1990).

Great sestinas are rare; the form, which works by repeating the same six line-endings in an elaborate pattern for six stanzas and a three-line coda, is often employed by novices who think it will be easy. They soon learn that sustaining such a poem requires diligence and skill. Hecht had already published a fine comedy in his "Sestina d'Inverno," so "The Book of Yolek" is partly his effort to prove he could be serious in the same form.

He begins with a meal "Of grilled brook trout" and a post-prandial walk, at which point "you remember, peacefully, an earlier day / In childhood, remember a quite specific meal. . . ." Notice that the form of address, the second person, implicates the reader or auditor in this ordinary experience. As the poem progresses, one of the end words, "to," will be varied as "1942" and then "tattoo," when another sort of camp is recalled, another manner of being lost, and another child, "Yolek who had bad lungs, who wasn't a day / Over five years old, commanded to leave his meal / And shamble between armed guards to his long home." The poem concludes as follows:

> Whether on that silent, solitary walk
> Or among crowds, far off or safe at home,
> You will remember, helplessly, that day,
> And the smell of smoke, and the loudspeakers of the camp.
> Wherever you are, Yolek will be there, too.
> His unuttered name will interrupt your meal.
>
> Prepare to receive him in your home some day.
> Though they killed him in the camp they sent him to,
> He will walk in as you're sitting down to a meal.

Anyone who thinks poetry has lost its power to ceremonialize our griefs, to astonish us with perennial relevance, has only to hear this poem to be persuaded otherwise. Its juxtaposition of civility and horror is particularly Hechtian. The same sort of juxtaposition is on display in poems like "A Hill," with its conclusion like an image out of Samuel Beckett, or in the humor and madness of "Third Avenue in Sunlight," or the mystery and manners of his poem about youthful sex, "The End of the Week-end." These are all titles from *The Hard Hours.* The title of his next book, *Millions of Strange Shadows,* was derived from Shakespeare's fifty-third sonnet: "What is your substance, whereof are you made, / That millions of strange shadows on you tend?" Despite the skepticism about appearance and reality throughout his work, this book is dedicated to Hecht's second wife, Helen, an assuredly beautiful presence in his happiest poems.

Our first glimpse of this willing suspension of disbelief comes in a blank verse monologue—one of several he published— called "Peripeteia." Readers may recall that the title is Aristotle's term for the initial phase of a tragic plot—the dramatic turn a play will take on its way to some discovery. Hecht's speaker begins in a theater with "the familiar rustling of programs, / My hair mussed from behind by a grand gesture / Of mink." This sense of social ostentation and self-consciousness is followed by a transitional state, the mind suspended, anticipatory, ruminative, and free. Then the play begins, and it is none other than *The Tempest,* a staged dream that counters the speaker's reverie and conquers it. Seeing the actress playing Miranda, the innocent capable of exclaiming "O brave new world," Hecht's speaker enters a new level of imaginative compulsion:

> . . . even she,
> Miraculous Miranda, steps from the stage,
> Moves up the aisle to my seat, where she stops,
> Smiles gently, seriously, and takes my hand
> And leads me out of the theatre, into a night
> As luminous as noon, more deeply real,
> Simply because of her hand, than any dream
> Shakespeare or I or anyone ever dreamed.

"Wait a minute!" most readers familiar with Hecht's usual nightmares will say. "How can he get away with this?" But he does, and his doing so is no small achievement. "Peripeteia" warns us about illusions while assenting to what might be illusory too, the love of that dream girl stepping off the stage. The poem is both an elaborate valentine to his wife and a wink and a nod to the rest of us, convincing because of its pace and detail.

Hecht was an astute observer of psychology; his poems are often as much about the action of the mind as the gestures of his protagonists. Soon after "Peripeteia" one finds "The Ghost in the Martini," a politically incorrect lyric about the male libido at work, written in witty stanzas. He heightens (or lowers?) the comedy by having the man's conscience speak from his drink as he is trying to seduce a younger woman.

My point in this hasty survey of the *Collected Earlier Poems* is to notice the deliberate way in which Hecht dramatized multiple aspects of human experience. He conveyed a surprising number of moods and social circumstances, few of them edifying. In the title poem of *The Venetian Vespers* his unnamed protagonist shares some of Hecht's war experience as well as his painterly use of words, modifiers daubed on like profligate brushstrokes. This highly unstable speaker, uncertain even of his own origins, ends up clinging to the visible world—"The soul being drenched in fine particulars"—as if for salvation.

When Hecht chooses protagonists further removed from himself he disturbs a kind of naturalistic decorum in which we are accustomed to fewer stylistic flourishes. Reading poems like "The Grapes" and "The Short End," I find myself torn. On the one hand, I sense of degree of condescension in Hecht's handling of "lower-class" subjects. On the other, I find the writing so accomplished, the poet's sympathy so genuine, that I'm almost completely won over.

Hecht's facility with multiple poetic modes—lyrics, meditations, narratives, satires and dramatic poems—continues in *Collected Later Poems*. In *The Transparent Man* two extended monologues, the title poem and "See Naples and Die," anchor the book with their fictional detail. If neither poem is quite so ambitious or moving as the character-driven work in *The Venetian Vespers,* each reconfirms Hecht's psychological range. A sequence I never adequately valued before called "A Love for Four Voices," in which the young lovers from *A Midsummer Night's Dream* make delightful speeches, now seems to me a successful Mozartian romp. Here Hecht indulged his affection for the Baroque, including such words as *cabochons* and *ipseity*. If there is any moral to this masque, perhaps it lies in a couplet spoken by Helena, observing that "If life is brief, . . . sex is even briefer, / Its joys like the illusions of a reefer. . . ." A few pages after "A Love for Four Voices" Hecht placed his elegy for David Kalstone, the critic "who died of AIDS." Again he alludes to Shakespeare: "'Men die from time to time,' said Rosalind, / 'But not,' she said, 'for love.' A lot she knew!" Again that counterpoint of voices. The "fine particulars" of Hecht's poems are forms of attention to the world's variety.

On longer acquaintance one becomes aware that Hecht's vision always had its moral—but never moralizing—aspect. He is convinced, like his speaker in "The Transparent Man," a woman dying of leukemia, that "the eye, self-satisfied, will be misled, / Thinking the puzzle solved, supposing at last / It can look forth and comprehend the world." People who think they know absolute truth become monsters of one sort or another. The very authority and apparent immodesty of Hecht's style are, in effect, a manifestation of his mistrust of conventional cant, part of his devotion to imaginative freedom even while accepting the restraints of rhetoric and poetic form. There's something anarchic in Hecht's vision that oddly verges on the surreal, but it's all so stylized and seemingly genteel that it sneaks up on you. He was a mannerist with good manners.

*Flight Among the Tombs,* the second volume in *Collected Later Poems,* begins with "The Presumptions of Death," a sequence treating Hecht's darker obsessions with brutal whimsy or arch civility, each poem accompanied by a woodcut from the late Leonard Baskin. Another poem, "The Mysteries of Caesar," portrays a Latin teacher whose tragedy was his closeted homosexuality. Still another high point in this volume is "Proust on Skates," imagining that utterly refined and isolated novelist enjoying ordinary sport. The poem finishes with a set of well-executed allusions to the life and work of its subject:

> It will not last, that happiness; nothing lasts;
> But will reduce in time to the clear brew
>       Of simmering memory
> Nourished by shadowy gardens, music, guests,
> Childhood affections, and, of Delft, a view
>       Steeped in a sip of tea.

The third and final book represented in this new collection is *The Darkness and the Light,* which I have reviewed elsewhere, commending again its range and particularly fine poems like "Sarabande on Attaining the Age of Seventy-Seven." It goes without saying that a man of Hecht's generation might have doubted he would survive his twenties, let alone live to an advanced age with continued productivity. The concluding stanza of Hecht's birthday gift to himself speaks for anyone who knows what being a survivor means:

> A turn, a glide, a quarter-turn and bow,
> The stately dance advances; these are airs
> Bone-deep and numbing, as I should know by now,
> Diminishing the cast like musical chairs.

Hecht's grand style, partly built upon revulsion at the worst humanity has to offer, partly upon the true poet's love of words and word-shapes, existed at a time when ornament of any sort was greeted with scorn or indifference. No other poet of Hecht's generation offered us such a range of characters, forms, elaborate and brutal forcefulness, yoking Europe and America in their joint experiences of art, war and the "wilderness of comfort" that is often our ordinary life. The modulated grace of Hecht's style might have prevented some readers from seeing how deeply he engaged with reality, even if he often expresses a Yeatsian desire for escape from that very reality. No other recent poet in English has fashioned such disillusioned beauty. What he once wrote for his dead friend Joseph Brodsky might well be said about Hecht's own work:

> Reader, dwell with his poems. Underneath
> Their gaiety and music, note the chilled strain
> Of irony, of felt and mastered pain,
> The sound of someone laughing through clenched teeth.

# Richard Wilbur and "The Blind Delight of Being"

Richard Wilbur is a great poet of dream and waking, the encoded world made articulate. In such well-known poems as "Love Calls Us to the Things of This World," the mystery of embodiment itself is at stake, and he carries this intense awareness in words even to his verses for children. Theorists may talk of "reading" the world, but no writer I can think of makes reading itself such a resonant metaphor for living. His *Collected Poems* (2004) begins with a recent example of blank verse, "The Reader," that evokes the whole project of literary involvement: "The blind delight of being, ready still / To enter life on life and see them through." It is also the perfect prologue to a volume containing the work of sixty years and an announcement of one of the poet's major themes, that *blind delight of being*. This poised opening both signals what will follow and eulogizes it, for what follows is the sort of poetry we are unlikely to meet again in our time.

Wilbur is the last of the "Big Three" of recent American poets, Donald Justice and Anthony Hecht having died. His living presence in the world of letters, and now the publication of his *Collected Poems,* is cause for acclamation. American poetry without Wilbur would be, in the words of his beloved Robert Frost, a diminished thing. Our literary horizon offers plenty of careerists to dominate an art of declining public importance, but few if any consummate makers who can offer the sort of enrichment Wilbur has given us.

He has never been the sort of formalist content to mass-produce the common fixed forms: sonnets, villanelles and sestinas. Nor has he been one for the large canvas, the epic or, as in James Merrill, dictation from the dead. What you get from

Wilbur is small-scale refinement, yet a lifetime of lyric-making on this order turns out to be more than it first appeared. Reviewing *Ceremony and Other Poems* (1950), Randall Jarrell was unimpressed:

> Richard Wilbur is a delicate, charming, and skillful poet. His poems not only make you use, but make you eager to use, words like attractive and appealing and engaging. . . . The reader notices that the poet never gets so lost either in his subject or in his emotions that he forgets to mix in his usual judicious proportion of all these things; his manners and manner never fail.

This dismissal of gentlemanliness came at roughly the moment when the barbaric yawp of confessional poetry was about to be sounded, not to mention Ginsberg's *Howl* and other self-important noises. The very reserve and quietude of Wilbur would seem, to some, anathema. He compounded the offense by not going crazy, leading an apparently happy life with a marriage of more than sixty years, and garnering a full slate of honors, including two Pulitzers. Where was the torment?

Jarrell looked for a more dramatic voice in the early poems, but despite the appearance of dramatic monologues (and dialogues) in subsequent volumes, Wilbur's theatrical talent would be largely relegated to the stage. His definitive translations of seventeenth-century French drama (Moliere, Racine, et al.) and his lyrics for Leonard Bernstein's *Candide* have apparently brought home the bacon since his retirement from teaching in 1986. This bourgeois success would not produce a poet of outrage, but a voice of civility. Like Poe he assumes that poetry is lessened the longer the poet goes on. Like Pope he adopts a public stance without placing himself at the center of things. His imagery is often suburban or rural, walled off from many of the issues that consume other contemporaries. Indeed, he mistrusts political pieties of any sort, finding a relatively modest role for the poet, perfecting his forms, many of them minted in the course of revision, discovered rather than borrowed from past writers.

Granted, then, Wilbur is not the narrative or dramatic poet Hecht was, nor a tormented megalomaniac like Lowell. That does not mean there are no sorrows in his life or work. It means that he has stubbornly transmuted tribulations into moments of grace, insisting that the world is more important than anything he can say about it. Here as evidence is a well-known short poem, first put between hard covers in 1987, "On Having Mis-Identified a Wild Flower":

> A thrush, because I'd been wrong,
> Burst rightly into song
> In a world not vague, not lonely,
> Not governed by me only.

Precisely because we don't govern the world, one has to accept Wilbur's conceit—the thrush's rebuke—with a nod and a wink. But what do his other terms suggest? *A world not vague:* that Darwinian impulse to assign names to things is a recognition of their ontology, isn't it? We're not alone in the world in both a biological and a religious sense, and Wilbur cannily refuses to accept one interpretation at the exclusion of the other. The very fact that he can be wrong in his reading of the world adopts humility without being pious about it, linking Wilbur's vision not only to Transcendentalists like Emerson, but also to such skeptical Christians as Eliot and Auden. (His debt to the knowledge games of Stevens and Frost is equally apparent.)

If Wilbur fundamentally celebrates the world rather than bemoaning it, perhaps this is because he has always felt our tenure here to be brief. We can see this in *The Beautiful Changes* (1947), where the title poem notices, "Your hands hold roses always in a way that says / They are not only yours. . . ." And we can see it in a later poem like "For W. H. Auden" (1987):

> Now I am surer where they were going,
> The brakie loping the tops of the moving freight,
> The beautiful girls in their outboard, waving to someone
> As the stern dug in and the wake pleated the water,
>
> The uniformed children led by a nun
> Through the terminal's uproar, the clew-drawn scholar descending
> The cast-iron stair of the stacks, shuffling his papers,
> The Indians, two to a blanket, passing in darkness,

> Also the German prisoner switching
> His dusty neck as the truck backfired and started—
> Of all these noted in stride and detained in memory
> I know better that they were going to die,
>
> Since you, who sustained the civil tongue
> In a scattering time, and were a poet of all our cities,
> Have for all your clever difference quietly left us,
> As we might have known that you would, by that common
>      door.

That common door is an Audenesque nod to poetry's place, not at the center of society but off to one side of it, the poet himself no more important or immune to death than any other citizen. The paradox of Wilbur's career has been that this maker of such finely wrought poems believes all poetry will *melt and go*. After all, his last discrete volume of poems and translations was called *Mayflies* (2000), after creatures that only live a day. The poignance of Wilbur's vision is that all art, whatever its strength, is pitted against extinction. And, whatever we believe, ultimately art and we will lose that battle. Of course he manages to forge moments of articulateness even for a time, but this gift makes the poet no more or less important than any other person who lives well, loves loyally and takes pleasure with Epicurean delight.

Born the son of a painter in New York City in 1921, Wilbur spent much of his childhood in what was then rural New Jersey. In a book-length interview with Peter Dale, he commented,

> My childhood left me with a preference for living in the sticks, for long walks, for physical work and the raising of great crops of herbs and vegetables. It made me a fair amateur naturalist and gave me an ability—essential in a poet, I should think—to make something of solitude.

As a young man his political leanings were "ordinary leftish ones, Rooseveltian and entirely patriotic," confirmed by a precollege year of tramping and rail-riding across nearly every state in the nation. That remarkable journey, alluded to in the first stanza of his Auden elegy above, is also the subject of a poem called, with typical irony, "Piccola Commedia."

Wilbur's politics almost got him into trouble when, after his marriage and graduation from Amherst College (B.A., 1942), he enlisted in the army's Thirty-sixth (Texas) Division. But the times were pressing, and when a division cryptographer went mad, Wilbur talked his way into the job, promising he had no intention of overthrowing the government. Critics have often remarked on the skill of cryptography in relation to Wilbur's love of old riddles and his adeptness with metaphor. Doubts occur about whether language—even as exacting as his—can accurately capture experience. Riddles are child's play with adult implications. One solves the mystery rather as one interprets the poem or gets the answer in class. For example, here is one of Wilbur's recent translations from the Latin of Symphosius: "To make men weep, though griefless, is my lot. / I seek to climb, but in damp air can not. / Without me, my begetter's not begot." The answer, given on another page, is *smoke*. So one sees how language and interpretation work in this game, but one is left still with all the unanswered riddles of existence—an absence in every poem. Of course, a wartime cryptographer's decoding skills would have a much more immediate purpose, potentially saving troops from enemy maneuvers. The poet's code-games are more beautiful, but their urgency is less absolute. Wilbur saw action in Italy and France, and would later attribute his first poems to such troubles: "One does not use poetry for its major purposes, as a means to organize oneself and the world, until one's world somehow gets out of hand."

Made order, then, the many shapes he would find for his poems, the fresh rhymes involving deep familiarity with the lexicon—all of these things are compensatory, and what we need to be compensated for is often implied rather than overtly stated.

After the war he did graduate study at Harvard, financed by that extraordinary boon, the G.I. Bill, then taught there, followed by a few years at Wellesley and twenty at Wesleyan University (1957–77), finishing with another ten years as writer-in-residence at Smith. With his wife, Charlee, he raised four children, one of whom "had the bad luck to be born autistic." The fact that Wilbur has not dwelt with a confessional poet's *Strum und Drang* on domestic difficulties sets him apart from his contemporaries. For a while there it seemed that bouts of madness and addiction were tickets to greatness, suicide merely the dues paid for one's laurels. If one lived dramatically, one wrote better. Not so, for Wilbur. Even the war gets scant notice in his work, especially if you compare him to James Dickey, Anthony Hecht, Louis Simpson and other soldier poets. In his first volume we do come across "Mined Country," "Potato," "First Snow in Alsace" and "On the Eyes of an SS Officer." But those poems are remarkable for their distance:

> Cows in mid-munch go splattered over the sky;
> Roses like brush-whores smile from bowers;
> Shepherds must learn a new language; this
> Isn't going to be quickly solved.

Like other intellectuals at war, he struggled to reconcile the pastoral trappings of his education with a world that could arbitrarily blow up in one's face.

His second book, *Ceremony*, which would be dissed by Jarrell, continued in the vein of deft irony, famously weighing the ordinary death of a toad "Toward some deep monotone, // Toward misted and ebullient seas / And cooling shores, toward lost Amphibia's emperies." The toad gets more baroque attention than the deaths of men witnessed in war, a fact which no doubt bothers some readers more than it does me. Wilbur was not telling war stories. Instead, he was a metaphysical poet, like Donne and Herbert in his lifelong obsession with last things, capable of extending complex metaphors, as in "Driftwood," the poem which follows "The Death of a Toad."

If critics like Jarrell can be excused for wondering whether there would be more, Wilbur's third book, *Things of This World* (1956), would, for all but the most uncharitable reader, confirm his intentions and accomplishments as a lyric poet. It also won him his first Pulitzer Prize. Like all of Wilbur's subsequent books, *Things of This World* mixed original poems with flawless translations. Its brilliance is best exemplified by the much-anthologized title poem, "Love Calls Us to the Things of This World" (a clause borrowed from St. Augustine), with its metaphysical play on angels and bed sheets. This is the poem that introduces us to a time of day, or of consciousness, that Wilbur would often revisit—the moment between sleep and waking, when we cannot help weighing one reality against another.

> The soul shrinks
>
> From all that it is about to remember,
> From the punctual rape of every blessèd day,
> And cries,
> "Oh, let there be nothing on earth but laundry,
> nothing but rosy hands in the rising steam
> and clear dances done in the sight of heaven."

The one proof-reading error I spotted in this new volume is a missed stanza break in this poem which, hopefully, will be corrected in later printings, honoring the care with which the poet has made his shapes.

Like Donne's, Wilbur's poetry would pit frank sensual pleasure against worldly pain and the intuition of something beyond us—death's other kingdom. Arguably such expert juxtapositions were there from the start in poems like "The Pardon," about the death of a boyhood pet. This is a poet who, in another early work, concluded, "I weary of the confidence of God"—hardly a small statement. But Wilbur's command was now even steadier, with no sign of the merely precious, even when he celebrated artifice in "A Baroque Wall-Fountain in the Villa Sciarra." As much as I love a handful of early Wilbur poems, it's from this point on that I feel he has really hit his stride. This is a poetry of civilized play, to be enjoyed as we enjoy any skillful artist in all his moods and modes. *Advice to a Prophet* (1961) and *Walking to Sleep* (1969) each collect poems and translations one would not want to miss, including yet another acknowledgment of horror, "On the Marginal Way":

> If these are bodies still,
> Theirs is a death too dead to look asleep,
> Like that of Auschwitz' final kill,
> Poor slaty flesh abandoned in a heap
> And then, like sea-rocks buried by a wave,
> Bulldozed at last into a common grave.

Compare this to Hecht's Holocaust poems, though, and you will see that horror is not Wilbur's metier.

*The Mind-Reader* (1976) contains in its title poem one of Wilbur's rare dramatic monologues, along with a group of his very best lyrics, including "The Writer," "To the Etruscan Poets," "Piccola Commedia" and "In Limbo." In "Cottage Street, 1953" Wilbur recounts a meeting with the young Sylvia Plath in which "It is my office to exemplify / The published poet in his happiness, / Thus cheering Sylvia, who has wished to die. . . ." The poem is Wilbur's mixed rejoinder to confessionalism and the cult of madness that swallowed up so many mid-century American poets. In it he admits not only the intelligence and power of Plath's "brilliant negative / In poems free and helpless and unjust," but also the insufficiency of his own response:

> I am a stupid life-guard who has found,
> Swept to his shallows by the tide, a girl
> Who, far from shore, has been immensely drowned,
> And stares through water now with eyes of pearl.

Only readers deaf to tonal nuance and complexity would say that Wilbur's poetry lacks passion. When in the same book he writes "For the Student Strikers" he responds to the passions surrounding the Kent State shootings, reminding us how easy it is to turn our fellow human beings into the enemy.

> It is not yet time for the rock, the bullet, the blunt
> Slogan that fuddles the mind toward force.
> Let the new sound in our streets be the patient sound
> Of your discourse.

Wilbur would not debase his art for easy sloganeering, and he took a lot of heat for advocating compassion "Even for the grey wife of your nightmare sheriff / And the guardsman's son." His rhyme of *force* and *discourse* is witty and incisive, because in our time Dionysian fury has too often trumped reasoned argument. For a poet to take this stance in 1970 was courageous, I think, just as it would be helpful now to find a political language that was not self-aggrandizing.

At that point in American history, and for nearly three subsequent decades, many American poets who shared Wilbur's esteem for measured speech, the viability of traditional techniques such as meter and rhyme, and a less egocentric stance, were dismissed in the most egregious and simplistic terms. Wilbur became for these poets—New Formalists and others—a paternal figure, a model of virtues that turn out to be worth having.

Wilbur's assertion of the power of articulateness makes him one of the most important writers to hear in our angry and divisive time. You can tell from his poems what his values are, but here they are restated in the Dale interview:

> Of course there are qualities, as opposed to whole persons, which I wholeheartedly dislike: mendacity, smugness, cruelty, stinginess, chic vulgarity. I find sanctimony and cocksure atheism equally disagreeable. Politically, my enemies are big-money Republicans, legislators who are essentially lobbyists, land speculators, ruthless entrepreneurs, generally.

If these values pit him against a large number of Americans, he is nevertheless not a simple-minded Liberal, precisely because of his capacity to doubt and his embrace of the Beatitudes, the private faith that underlies his public voice.

*New and Collected Poems* (1987) won a second Pulitzer for Wilbur and, in its previously uncollected poems, included such masterpieces as "The Ride" and "Hamlen Brook," the latter ending

> Joy's trick is to supply
> Dry lips with what can cool and slake,
> Leaving them dumbstruck also with an ache
> Nothing can satisfy.

I don't know a better stanza about poetry than this one, which builds on the image of a minnow in a stream "Trawling a shadow solider than he." Poetry is joy's trick—that transforming gaiety of art Yeats wrote about. It does slake a kind of thirst we may not always be aware of suffering, but it does not cure us of our ills or remove us from essential trials and responsibilities. Its solace is temporary.

Like Auden, Wilbur places the onus for living not on the literary artifact but on the reader and the poet. That is why his poems rejoice in family life, and here his long marriage to a woman who loves poetry with an earthly delight becomes a sustaining image. In *Mayflies* he printed his homage to that marriage and that woman, "For C." He begins by considering those who have led more conventionally passionate lives, having love affairs or otherwise caught up in the sexual revolution, and concludes as follows:

> We are denied, my love, their fine tristesse
> And bittersweet regrets, and cannot share
> The frequent vistas of their large despair,
> Where love and all are swept to nothingness;
> Still, there's a certain scope in that long love
> Which constant spirits are the keepers of,
>
> And which, though taken to be tame and staid,
> Is a wild sostenuto of the heart,
> A passion joined to courtesy and art
> Which has the quality of something made,
> Like a good fiddle, like the rose's scent,
> Like a rose window or the firmament.

I doubt a poet's spouse or partner has ever been the excuse for a more transcendent lyric. One can point to weaknesses in Wilbur's oeuvre: a tendency to sound at times like channeled Frost, a slightness in some of the early poems, a relatively narrow range of dramatic voices. But when he speaks with full eloquence, we have no better poet in America.

One of Wilbur's best dramatic gifts is his ability to write for children, and the new volume does us an immense favor by reprinting the complete texts of *Opposites, More Opposites, A Few Differences, The Disappearing Alphabet* and *The Pig in the Spigot,* some of them illustrated with the poet's own Thurberesque drawings. In recent years, Wilbur has concluded public readings with excerpts from *The Disappearing Alphabet,* bringing down the house and leaving his audience with a champagne giddiness:

Because they're always BUZZING, honey bees
Could not be with us if there were no Z's,
And many Z's are needed, furthermore,
When people feel the need to SNOOZE and snore.
Long live the Z, then! Not for any money,
Would I give up such things as sleep and honey.

Once you finish laughing, you might think through the poem's dependence on our alphabet and an English vocabulary, realizing that Wilbur the riddler is playing with you, turning ideas about word and world into yet another game as deftly as any postmodernist.

Wilbur's stanzaic inventiveness has much to teach new poets who are at times too content merely to reproduce received forms. But he is also one of the best teachers for poets of shapeless rage, asking all of us to calm down and look harder for the right words. His metaphysical bent is tragi-comic, torn between belief and doubt as it is between sleep and waking. He is a poet of consciousness, of mind, who would agree with that other poet of mind, Wallace Stevens, that "The greatest poverty is not to live / In a physical world." If one of poetry's functions is to help us awaken more fully into our lives, Wilbur has made this his great subject. He is our cultivated guide to mysteries of our own incarnations, our own blind delight of being.

# Grace Schulman's Song of Praise

The power of the visible
is the invisible.
—Marianne Moore

Midway through her critical study *Marianne Moore: The Poetry of Engagement* (1986), Grace Schulman recalls a visit to the older poet's home in 1968. There they spoke about a poem in which Moore had written,

> I am hard to disgust,
> but a pretentious poet can do it;
> a person without a taproot; and
> impercipience can do it; did it.

Schulman relates the image of that taproot to Moore's "poetics of growth by perceptual change." The organic metaphor is a meeting of world and mind. "A taproot," Moore said in conversation, "is the center of a plant that is firm in the ground. I don't like a person with no idea, with mercurial comings and goings, one who says, 'Are you going to a concert? Oh, I think I'll go too.' That person is always shaping his actions to what someone else is doing."

It would be eight years before Schulman published her first full-length collection of poems, *Burn Down the Icons* (1976), with its title suggesting more a clean slate than a rooted plant, but if I may borrow Moore's metaphor, Schulman has been a person with a taproot. She has always been a poet with a sense of place, particularly New York City. Her poems are rooted in that city's present and its past. Like someone hearing footsteps and looking under her own soles to see what is there, she is sensitive to echoes of other times and people. The taproot of her poetry is severally fed, nourished by other minds and other peoples' art, and this consciousness also implies what is beyond poetry, the names we know only by their absence or by our ignorance of them. For Schulman the poet is not exactly the namer in Emerson's sense, but the namer in a fallen world, approaching what cannot be named. Schulman's rootedness and percipience are the sources of a lifelong song of praise. The terms of her belief are often richly traditional—here I refer both to her sources and her verse forms—but informed as well by the experience of human limitation. The poet names, unnames and names again, but these visions and revisions are a rooted tribute to existence even in its trials.

Already I am bound to paradox. How can something be singular and multiple at the same time? A taproot with many roots? Footsteps and echoes of footsteps? I can only reply that Grace Schulman is a kind of metaphysical poet, in both her meditative strategies and the religious nature of her argument. Outside of the poems themselves, one place to begin understanding her vision is her critical essay "The Persistence of Tradition," published in *Where We Stand: Women Poets on Literary Tradition* (1993). Here she names three principal influences on her life and art: Walt Whitman, Henry James, and her grandfather, "a Hungarian-born Jewish immigrant." She is particularly concerned with passages in which James and Whitman write about the culture of her grandfather as found in lower Manhattan in the nineteenth century. These divergent literary artists observed the vital transformation of New York due to immigration, and in Whitman's case at least, the influence was profound—this despite his ignorance of Jewish religion. Schulman quotes from a newspaper article in which Whitman describes Jewish ritual without being able to name it, then briefly traces the literary influence of translated Hebrew poetry upon Whitman's style.

Her point is simple: we are influenced by more than is immediately apparent to us—more than we can name.

As I write this now, I am surrounded by cultures, all of them beautiful. Without getting up from my desk I can see, on the shelves around me, a new translation of the *Gilgamesh*, by David Ferry; an anthology of Chinese poetry edited by Donald

Finkel; Lu Chi's *Wen Fu,* a new translation by Sam Hamill; William Matthews' versions of Martial in his *Selected Poems and Translations;* anthologies of Russian poetry and of African poetry; and a programme from the Barbican Theatre in London, for Sophocles' Theban trilogy in a new translation by Timberlake Wertenbaker, and with choric dances that include, appropriately, African and Asian dances that may have informed ancient drama.

Tradition, then, is not the looming edifice some take it to be, but a swarm of echoes like footsteps on a New York street. Schulman's New York, so clearly made by physical inhabitants, is also a New York of ideas, words, images. It's the city of glass and brick mentioned so often in her poems, but also the urban garden with its small suggestions of another garden long ago.

In 1994, writing about the poetry of May Swenson, Schulman again rethought the image of Adam's naming: "The poet's unnaming allows her to rename, in an effort to see things outside the context of common parlance." Naming and unnaming are frequent tropes in Schulman's poems precisely because she apprehends the unnamable.

> To see in the dark
> the south window strew flowers
>
> on the chapel floor,
> or wind peel a sand rose,
>
> is unnamable,
> like joy,
>
> like my love's grin
> between a cap and a jacket.
>
> Names are for things
> we cannot own.

These lines conclude a poem called "Eve's Unnaming." And what an intriguing suggestion—that we can somehow "own" the joy we cannot name. You can see here the complex equivalence Schulman fashions between experience and belief, mortality and intimations of the immortal. This essentially religious vision, quizzical and unburdened by the more simplistic pieties, is informed by Schulman's variegated sense of tradition, both in art and in the immediate experience of immigrants, particularly in her family. It is Jewish but somehow ecumenical, resembling her library of books. It is local, rooted in New York, but full of the diverse echoes one hears in such a city of the world.

I would argue that Schulman's work in five collections of poems from 1976 to the present year (2002) is utterly consistent in its ideas and beliefs, even as it follows her growth, the increasing confidence of her technique and strength of her vision. She has become a taproot poet, not only of New York City, but also of the twin human needs, to lament and praise.

ঽ৶

Part of the consistency of Schulman's vision is its tremor of doubt, an intuition that human beings are born divided and incapable of whole sight except in glimmerings. Her early poem "Double Vision," which she chose not to include in the most recent selection of her work, seems to me important at least as an evolutionary step:

> In that place there are no atlases,
> No lighthouses, no laws. No gravity.
> The saints unsanctified,
> My language lies undone.
>
> My arms are seared with numbers and my hands
> Detonate when they reach out.
> Circles read "You Are Here"—there.
>
> It is a black arrow trembling in a yellow diamond;
> "What is it?" he screamed, his eyes were fallen rocks;
> "Danger," I replied.
> "You're wrong," he said. "It is an arrow."
>
> Dreamless I ran unsteadied in that night
> And prayed for tolerant winds to sing me home,
> But I would set my stores by that disordered ocean.
>
> Eyes be my images
> O fire I fear
> I am the star in the East
> I rise in dry places and fall knowing

> My heart's arhythmia, my double vision
> Are handicaps. They are all I have.
> I am at the bottom of that rock
> From which altars are built.

I suppose I can see why she chose not to include this poem. One might say it gets melodramatic: "My arms are seared with numbers and my hands / Detonate when they reach out." But Schulman's father was a Polish émigré who escaped before the Holocaust, and one aunt was actually shot during the Warsaw uprising of 1943. Schulman's poems are frequently imprinted by history, which is always both personal and public. One of her recent poems, "1932," details a visit her father made to the coastal city of Danzig, which some of us know as Gdansk, where he showed the old country to his American bride. The poem concludes with a plea: "Don't stay in Germany! / Come back on the last ship. Let me be born."

But the earlier poem, "Double Vision," is about another country as well—a land of slippery signifiers. A "he" and an "I" who inhabit the poem differ about how they read these signs, and here I recall both "Eve's Unnaming" and "The Examination: Remembrance of Words Lost," an apparently autobiographical poem in which Schulman discovers herself as a poet partly by losing the ability to speak in a Ph.D. exam. "Double Vision" is about being handicapped in one sense, gifted in another. "I am at the bottom of that rock / From which altars are built," she concludes, echoing Rilke's *Sonnets to Orpheus,* and one could well argue that Schulman has been building a sort of altar ever since, her *Days of Wonder: New and Selected Poems* (2002) comparable to George Herbert's *The Temple,* a seventeenth-century book of lyric poems that are often engaged in argument with the Almighty.

Schulman's religious vision cannot be understood, I think, without this sense of human dividedness and limitation. The poem immediately following "Double Vision" in her first book is called "Lost Unity"—as if Grace Schulman could not help being conscious of a fall from Grace. But that book contains a lyric called "Surely as Certainty Changes" offering images of wholeness as well:

Surely as certainty changes,
As tide moves sand,
As heat sends wind to force the sea into waves,
As water rises and returns in rain
Or circles into smoke and falls in vapor,
You are enchanted for you enter change
And change is holy.

As earth's weight compresses rocks
Under trees over time, you enter change,
I know your face gives light as I know fire
Alters everything,
And falls rising,
Feeds and nourishes, opens and closes.

I pray to Proteus, the god of change
And proteolysis, "the end of change
Changing in the end"
To break old images and make you new
As love is its own effect unendingly.

To enter change is to be enchanted, and enchantment—as she
reminds us in her book on Moore—has its root in song, which
embodies an exalted state and is paradoxical. Schulman's icon-
oclasm in this first book is a way of unnaming and renaming creation, a groping toward praise. It's notable, too, that this poet
long married to a scientist would use the term *proteolysis*, having
to do with the dissolution of proteins, in a love poem about un-
ending change. One of her most endearing characteristics as a
poet is her humility, a willingness to look at the world outside
herself with an almost scientific inquisitiveness.

Schulman's second book, *Hemispheres* (1984), extends her
paradoxical vision. Poems like "Borders" and "Division" deal
with strife, but the book begins with "Blessed is the Light," a
praise song that echoes Whitman echoing the Bible. "Let There
Be Translators!" evokes division in the story of Babel, but also
the human apprehension of wholeness in that noble effort to
communicate the experience of other people in other tongues.
The title poem, "Hemispheres," suggests Aristophanes's tale of
the Hermaphrodites as given by Plato in the Symposium, where

love is a search for unity of being, just as in poetry, just as in prayer. Another short poem, "Losses," briefly expresses the paradox Schulman has limned from the start, and here I can't help noticing a debt to another visionary poet, Theodore Roethke:

> Life's gains are losses: water leeches rock,
> rivers erode and deltas restore the land;
> the sun melts ice, turns rain to clouds of mist.
> Wind spins palms in circles like propellers
> Squanders its force; the fire that feeds destroys.

If, as I argue, Schulman's work is a polytonal song of praise, it is also coherent and complex in its intellectual lineaments. Her third book, *For That Day Only* (1994), contains a poem entitled "The Ter Clos" in which a literal absence or aporia becomes an imaginary presence. Like Elizabeth Bishop's "The Man Moth," "The Ter Clos" is a poem derived from error. Bishop's was a newspaper misprint for "Mammoth," and she imagined a creature not unlike the Hunchback of Notre Dame tearfully clinging to the sides of buildings—an image of a misfit, perhaps playfully autobiographical. Schulman's *ter clos,* a note tells us, was born when a sign that read "Theater Closed" lost some of its letters. So, from an emblem of stifled imagination, an erasure, a new being is born:

> Just before dawn,
> the *ter clos* unfolds metal legs and slides
> down from its canopy and tells of scenes
> played and replayed; a dancer glides;
> a brigantine
> dips in the ocean. . . .

This creature's consciousness is the universe of images that have flickered on a screen in a dark theater. It is not willing to hear of another creation—the one beyond human artifice—and the poem concludes,

> The *ter clos* fumes
> at the story of the world's beginning:
> of how God hushed his coloratura thrones,

his mezzo archangels, to hear men, women—
his creatures—sing,
sometimes off-tune.

Grotesque as it appears, the *ter clos* is a creature of artificial
beauty that cannot stomach human imperfection. Schulman's
poem is not, like Bishop's, a surreal image of the isolated soul,
so much as it is like William Butler Yeats's "The Dolls," a meditation on making, raising questions about plans and accidents,
perfection and frailty, and whether any sort of creation can be
called permanent.

❧

*For That Day Only,* like *Hemispheres,* was an advance over earlier
work, and both books demonstrated that Schulman was contin-
ually refining her art and ideas. One of the most significant
poems in *For That Day Only* is "Footsteps on Lower Broadway,"
which in part led her to compose the essay I alluded to earlier,
"The Persistence of Tradition." It begins with grace, the image of
Grace Church that was seen by both Whitman and Henry James,
and quickly summons up her grandfather, "a Jew / who read the
law and knew the ritual." The poem is a sort of extended ballade,
its rhymes occasionally slant or disguised by enjambment, its
refrain modulated. This sense of formal pattern, clearly present
but disguised, is a successful embodiment of the poem's idea
that existence is patterned, though we might perceive little of its
shape. Schulman has always been eclectic in her techniques,
never a poet to fall into a formal or rhetorical rut, and this may
in part be due to her studies of such poets as Pound and Moore.
But I am reminded of another New Yorker, a transplanted
one—W. H. Auden. In this case it's less the tone or the voice
that reminds me of another poet than the ideas. The guiding
trope or cynosure of Auden's intellectual universe was the Fall
from Grace. In poem after poem he maps this land of unlike-
ness, of alienated people, lovers who cannot save each other or
themselves, the insufficiency of politics and philosophy before
that silence he called the Wrath of God. Auden reminds us that
birth itself, the exit wailing from the womb, is a manifestation of
the Fall. If you'll allow a whimsical aside, I also recall Auden's

friend Cyril Connelly writing that we are "all our lives seeking a womb with a view." The womb and the garden are lost to us, though—at least for permanent residency—and our burden of responsibility for living is a heavy one. This helps to explain Auden's struggle toward religious belief. I am also fond of noticing that poetry itself is a manifestation of the Fall. Language becomes more necessary to us the further we're removed from the Mother.

Schulman's poem "Notes from Underground: W. H. Auden on the IRT" acknowledges a kinship with that great poet:

> His eyes lifted over my tattered copy
> of his *Selected Poems,* then up to where
> they drilled new windows in the car and found,
> I guessed, tea roses and a healing fountain.

The poem's act of homage signals a reader fond of such connections to think about Auden's influence upon Schulman. Like Moore, Auden gave her permission to be formally and intellectually exacting, personal but also percipient about the world outside herself, its history and biology—to be a poet of ideas and not merely autobiography. The image she gives us of herself in this poem is of someone who retires into reading, who inhabits an underground of her own, and here I think of the particular kinds of service Schulman has given the literary world, directing the Poetry Center of the 92nd Street Y for a decade, and serving still as poetry editor for the *Nation,* a magazine that published Moore and Auden. I don't happen to know whether she's as shy as the poem suggests, but the work displays a consistent displacement of the self, an unwillingness to stand center stage without putting other people forward, and this too I find attractive.

Schulman's fourth book, *The Paintings of Our Lives* (2001), continues this juxtaposition of Truth with our representations and readings of it, but it also risks the most powerful emotions of any of her books so far, especially in its concluding sequence of sonnets, "One Year Without Mother." If you take up the themes and ideas I have been tracing so far—our fragmentation and search for Grace, the dialectic of life and art, unnaming and naming, lamentation and praise—you will find them beautifully extended here, as you will in the new poems collected at the back of *Days of Wonder* (2002).

*The Paintings of Our Lives* begins with a *ghazal*, a poem in the medieval Persian form recently popularized in America by the late Agha Shahid Ali, a Pakistani by birth. Schulman's "Prayer" resurrects the image of another city that recurs in her work for obvious reasons, Jerusalem, and here Schulman continues to hope, as we all do, for a healing of divisions. She alludes to Ali's work translating the Israeli poet Judah Halevi, and the fact that she herself is using a form associated with Islamic civilization does not no unnoticed. "My name is Grace," she concludes, "Chana in Hebrew—and in Arabic. / May its meaning, 'God's Love,' at last be taught in Jerusalem." This is a book, in other words, in which art and prayer contend equally with a divided world and seek healing or wholeness. It is also a book in which one can see Schulman's quiet feminist consciousness at work, as in "Young Woman Drawing, 1801." A note tells us that the painting depicted in this poem was originally attributed to Jacques Louis David, then changed to "Constance Charpentier, and, most recently, to Marie-Denise Villers, 1774–1821." It observes a young artist as well as what she observes of life, and it begins, "Subject and maker shed their names. . . ." We have an unnaming Eve again, the emphasis of art placed on the experience we can never quite name. Add the act of reading and interpreting to this process, and you can see that Schulman tweaks not only the men who misattributed the painting, but also anyone who views it, even the subject's view of other subjects.

Another poem, "Margaret Fuller," recalls the pioneering feminist and woman of letters who drowned in a shipwreck off Fire Island in 1850. Fuller's life was full of dividedness, even when she found substantial success as a writer and editor. A Cambridge transcendentalist, she edited the *Dial* from 1840 until 1842— the very journal that in a revived version would be edited by Marianne Moore. Toward the end of her short life Fuller went to Rome, married an Italian aristocrat, the Marchese Giovanni Ossoli, and took part in the revolution of 1848–49. Her husband and infant son died with her in the wreck as they attempted to return to America. For Schulman, this dramatic life and death are emblematic of what I can only call the human condition.

Fuller was, like all of us except perhaps some of the saints, a divided soul. Dying, she "lost her torn self to the sea's wholeness." The poem's speaker has tried to reach Fuller, swum out perhaps like the poet's mind trying to reach across time. Schulman isn't rescued by faith from any of life's difficulties. I'm reminded of Auden again, who, echoing Kierkegaard, wrote,

> A solitude ten thousand fathoms deep
> Sustains the bed on which we lie, my dear.
> Although I love you, you will have to leap.
> Our dream of safety has to disappear.

There is also a touching remembrance of the critic Irving Howe and a fine poem about Henry James revisiting Washington Square—both poems in which a diurnal setting offers suggestions of timelessness, like that image of the sea in "Margaret Fuller." The book's title poem begins with *The Annunciation Triptych* housed in the Cloisters at the north end of Manhattan—yet another image of the eternal entering the ordinary, and Mary does not even notice the approaching angel Gabriel. "Somewhere are the paintings of our lives," Schulman writes, "—invisible to us. . . ." We're like those books she neglected to name from her library, real and even minutely influential whether anyone names us or not.

The sonnet sequence, "One Year Without Mother," could be compared to Seamus Heaney's "Clearances," both as a portrayal of a parent after her death and as a confident use of the form. Heaney had learned from Frost and Kavanagh and perhaps Louis MacNeice how to get character across in little gestures, and Schulman's sequence has such moments—for example the fourth sonnet, "Ceremony":

> To put your house in order, I went back
> more than I had to, polished a decanter,
> hoisted a painting with your self-stick stuck
> behind, "a real "Gekko," and scrubbed silver
>
> for unknown others. Needless labor, yet
> my privilege: nine women washed Schmuel,
> my ancestor, then swaddled him for burial.
> A daughter's right. Her rite. How rites persist

> when prayer comes hard. My husband's faith, hard-won,
> is only that the genome project may
> restore the sick. But last year, at the cemetery,
> I watched him twist a shovel spade-side down
> in a half-remembered ritual, and then
> dig it in earth he scattered on your coffin.

It's a poem about tradition that persists whether we know it or not, and by extension it's about all those hard survivals from every nation on earth that have made America. We have lamentation, as in the twelfth sonnet, which offers images of "turbulent life" on a Greek funeral urn. We have a sonnet called "Credo" that ends, "Hosannas, kaddish, Oms, sing on my pages, / hold back the dark, help me live out my days." And in the final sonnet, "Requiem," we have two words offered in both accusation and inspiration: "Praise life."

 za.

This is a very good year to be giving the Aiken-Taylor Award to Grace Schulman, not only for her years of service to the art, but also to mark the publication of *Days of Wonder: New and Selected Poems,* a book that is both the culmination of a superb poet's work so far and an affirmation of faith as it "crushes / and builds"—unnames and names. This book contains ten new poems, including two—"Flags" and "1932"—that deal openly with anti-Semitism, and a marvelous lyric about faith called "Job's Question on Nevis." Here we find a woman on the Caribbean island of that name who has apparently experienced ruinous storms, racism, and poverty, and asks like Job, "Will the Almighty answer me?"

> Silent, I watched her. Under a blank sky,
> where waves broke over coral, in thick haze,
> pitched forward to hear the whirlwind's reply,
> she shook a fist, then opened hands in praise.

Grace Schulman's days of wonder can be hard days, Job-like days, but her steady voice will not tolerate self-pity. Maybe, as Marianne Moore wrote, "The power of the visible / is the invisible." Maybe the reverse is true. We can't know. And this poetry is about our being here and not being able to know, and deciding to sing in spite of it.

# Memory and Imagination in the Poetry of B. H. Fairchild

Let me begin with two errors. The first is my own in the title, which suggests that memory and imagination are separable. In fact, the underlying supposition of this essay will be closer to the meaning Thomas Hobbes gave these terms in *Leviathan:*

> This *decaying sense,* when we would express the thing itself . . . we call *imagination* . . . ; but when we would express the decay and signify that the sense is fading, old, and past, it is called *memory.* So that imagination and memory are but one thing, which for divers considerations has divers names.

Maybe in English we need a new word—*mémagination.* Just as the Greek word for a novel, *mythistorema,* combines both myth and history, our word would mix memory and imagination.

I raise this issue at the outset because of the second error, sometimes made by critics reading the poems of B. H. Fairchild, too simplistically calling him a poet of memory. The poet is either virtuous or not (depending on what sort of axe the critic grinds), precisely because his poems enact memories of his working-class youth. Never mind that Fairchild's family aspired to the middle class; the fact of a blue-collar environment confuses matters of money and social situation. Work is virtue; wealth is criminal. Fairchild gets lumped with Philip Levine (also piously misread) as a poet of the underclass, sometimes accused of sentimentality for giving us images like old W.P.A. photographs depicting noble poverty. My contention here is simply that Fairchild is far more thoughtful, far more complicated a writer than many critics have yet understood. He is a philosophical poet whose ideas are embodied in narratives about a variety of people, often skilled laborers whose work parallels the achievements of artists and athletes. These poems are imagined as much as remembered; they are shaped not only as lyric performances, but also as sketches and full-fledged stories or meditations. Narratives, I should add, are every bit as formal as sonnets or villanelles. Even before they are written they have a shape, like some small, wholly formed object you can put in your pocket or turn in the palm of your hand. Narrative is too often perceived as the property of prose writers, when in many ways poets are the ideal storytellers because they work close to the bones and sinews of language. Fairchild has thought long and hard about storytelling in verse, and this, too, is part of the vitality of his poems.

Some of our best poets are misread as untutored country bumpkins—I think of Robert Frost and our recent poet laureate, Ted Kooser. A certain kind of critic looks for obvious signs of erudition, approving especially of formal difficulty or theoretical arcana. Fairchild seems easy to lump in with other Midwestern regionalists. This perception of the cultural periphery, sustained by perceived cultural centers, conflates manual labor and simple-mindedness. However, a second glance will show even the most thick-headed critic that Fairchild rarely writes poems about blue-collar people alone. Almost everything he has published is self-consciously artful or *about* art or about people for whom art plays some important role.

His first book of poems, *The Arrival of the Future* (published in 1985 and reprinted in 2000), is utterly deliberate in its organization. The opening poem, "Machine Shop with Wheat Field," is a painterly depiction of a work-space within a wide open landscape—almost a Renaissance painter's sense of shapes and spatial relationships. This is followed by a poem called "The Men"—and indeed, notions of masculinity and male grief will be important themes throughout his work. But Fairchild follows "The Men" with "Angels," and the implications of this juxtaposition deepen when we turn to the poem itself:

## Angels

Elliot Ray Neiderland, home from college
one winter, hauling a load of Herefords
from Hogtown to Guymon with a pint of
Ezra Brooks and a copy of Rilke's *Duineser
Elegien* on the seat beside him, saw the ass-end
of his semi gliding around in the side mirror
as he hit ice and knew he would never live
to see graduation or the castle at Duino.

In the hospital, head wrapped like a gift
(the nurses had stuck a bow on top), he said
four flaming angels crouched on the hood, wings
spread so wide he couldn't see, and then
the world collapsed. We smiled and passed a flask
around. Little Bill and I sang *Your Cheatin'
Heart* and laughed, and then a sudden quiet
put a hard edge on the morning and we left.

*Siehe, ich lebe,* Look, I'm alive, he said,
leaping down the hospital steps. The nurses
waved, white dresses puffed out like pigeons
in the morning breeze. We roared off in my Dodge,
*Behold, I come like a thief!* he shouted to the town
and gave his life to poetry. He lives, now,
in the south of France. His poems arrive
by mail, and we read them and do not understand.

Now, what are we to make of a poem alluding to Rilke, Hank Williams and the Book of Revelation? First, that Fairchild denies us the stereotypical class distinctions in which blue-collar workers are patronized as semi-literate citizens. Elliot Ray Neiderland, a forerunner to later Fairchild characters like Travis Doyle and Roy Garcia, is a college boy making his living by driving a cattle truck—just as I myself worked as a manual laborer well into my thirties while pursuing the career of a writer and educator. Fairchild knows that education is not exclusively the province of white-collar suburbia, and some criticisms of his poetry—notably a review by William Logan in the *New Criterion*—reveal a sort of bigotry about class in America, a prejudice this poetry shrugs off like a minor irritation.

This early poem already shows us a poet with sure narrative instincts. There's that long sentence, comprising the whole opening stanza, in which we quickly learn who this guy is, where he is, that both booze and German poetry are part of his life, and that he has found himself skidding on the ice, doing a comic double-take as he watches the jackknifed trailer pass the cab of his truck. In the second stanza we get those enjoyable details about the head bandaged "like a gift" with "a bow on top" put there by the nurses. We get his hallucinated angels—booze and poetry having done their dirty work—in contrast to the very real and very good-humored nurses. And we get the sobering effect of the Hank Williams song, though why those lines about adultery "put a hard edge on the morning" we are not informed. Then, marvelously, the poem leaps into the future, and none of Elliot Ray Neiderland's motives are explained. Does he run off to France to become a poet out of gratitude at finding himself alive? Is he a very good poet? Has he gone mad? None of these questions are answered. We only know that the speaker stays in touch, receives the poems by mail, but does not understand them.

This poem's mystery of men and angels, presence and absence, being and non-being, stems from Fairchild's immersion in philosophy as well as poetry. What I most urgently want to underline about his achievement is not only that he gives voice to characters who might be incapable of such eloquence on their own behalf, but also that his poems display a voracious intellectual life, a synthetic sensibility that refuses to separate such things as Renaissance art and baseball, jazz and poetry, or to deny the reality of the cultural periphery as well as the cultural center.

*The Arrival of the Future* borrows from such minds as George Steiner, George Oppen, Charles Olson, Wolfgang Pannenburg and Ludwig Wittgenstein, the latter providing this epigraph: "The limits of my language are the limits of my world." Fairchild seems to have been drawn instinctively to philosophies of language, especially to the ideas of Martin Heidegger. Discussing Rilke's *Sonnets to Orpheus*, Heidegger had written, "To sing the song means to be present in what is present itself. It means: *Dasein*, existence." The work of art signifies such presence, but also an implied absence, a sort of *via negativa* through which we understand what it is to be alive in the world. For Heidegger, the poetic is prior to the poem itself. We come to language out of desire, and "man creates poetry from the very nature of the poetic." This philosophical sympathy for the poetic mode of being distinguishes Heidegger from, say, the Plato of the *Republic*. For Heidegger, poetry is not an escape, but (to use Auden's phrase) "a way of happening." In *Poetry, Language, Thought*, Heidegger wrote:

> Poetry does not fly above and surmount the earth in order to escape it and hover over it. Poetry is what first brings man onto the earth, making him belong to it, and thus brings him into dwelling.

These ideas are not easy to understand—at least not for me—and I don't mean to suggest more equanimity in Fairchild than is actually there. He has had his trials. Born in Texas in 1942, the poet grew up in small towns there and in Oklahoma and Kansas. He got his degrees at the Universities of Kansas and Tulsa, and often supported himself as a young man by working in his father's machine shop as well as at other jobs before becoming an academic. In an afterword to his second collection, *Local Knowledge*, Fairchild remembers his father at work:

> In machine shops in Houston, Lubbock, Midland, and Snyder, Texas, I would as a boy stand on the wooden ramp next to my father and watch his hands move gracefully and efficiently over the lathe, maneuvering the levers and rotary handles and making the bit move in and out, back and forth, as the huge chuck spun a section of drill pipe in its iron grip. Once he had the bit set just right, having measured the cut with the calipers, he would let go, and a steady spiral of blue steel shaving would coil out into the darkness, dropping with a hiss into the milky mixture of oil and water below. He would then lean back, light a cigarette, pour himself a cup of coffee, and breathe slowly in that easy, contented way of someone sure of his craft.

The parallels with poetry are obvious here, and eventually Fairchild would make more of them, more of the ontological awareness of work. He would do this because he was an American provincial who wanted more. I'm a provincial fellow myself, and I think I understand that desire to connect the details of remembered life with a more expansive vision. It's the desire of a poet, who feels somehow orphaned or set apart from his surroundings by his peculiar affections, to be adopted by the larger world, or to be worthy of such adoption.

But this process starts with local knowledge. That and reading. Fairchild has said that one of the richer reading experiences of his youth was Ernest Thompson Seton's *The Biography of a Grizzly* (1900). My own copy of this book was reprinted by the Boy Scouts of America, and I remember being gripped by its evocation of a bear's life from a bear's point of view. I've re-read the book recently, noting the extended pathos of its closing pages as Wahb grows old, loses strength and, feeling his many wounds, gradually abandons his territory:

> And feeling, as far as a Bear can feel, that he is fallen, defeated, dethroned at last, that he is driven from his ancient range by a Bear too strong for him to face, he turned up the west fork, and the lot was drawn.

Wahb's struggle is a particular thing, but perhaps in Fairchild's imagination it was associated with the trials of the men he knew in machine shops, men who felt an absence or a failure they could not express. In Fairchild's poems they are vigorous, they are fighters and sportsmen, and some of them have great dignity, but their lives are losing battles because they measure themselves against something greater, an almost unplumbed aesthetic sense or ineffable desire.

> I see them in their little white frame houses on the edge
> of town adrift in the long silence of the evening turning
> finally to their wives, touching without speaking the hair
> which she has learned to let fall about her shoulders
> at this hour of night, lifting the white nightgown
> from her body as she in turn unbuttons his work shirt
> heavy with the sweat and grease of the day's labor until
> they stand naked before each other and begin to touch
> in a slow choreography of familiar gestures their bodies,
> she touching his chest, his hand brushing her breasts,

and he does not say the word "beautiful" because
he cannot and never has, and she does not say it
because it would embarrass him or any other man
she has ever known. . . .

They are not unlike the poet, of course, and he knows this. The bond Fairchild feels with his people is what gives so much of his work its gravity.

In his most recent book Fairchild uses another of his favorite reads—James Agee's *A Death in the Family*—as an organizing text. The long epigraph includes these words:

May God bless my people, my uncle, my aunt, my mother, my good father, Oh, remember them kindly in their time of trouble; and in the hour of their taking away.

After a little I am taken in and put to bed. Sleep, soft smiling, draws me unto her: and those who receive me, who quietly treat me, as one familiar and well-beloved in that home: but will not, oh, will not, not now, not ever; but will not ever tell me who I am.

These readings are full of that "pleasing anxious being" at the heart of poetry, that verbal awareness. Not only novels and philosophical ruminations lie beneath Fairchild's work. He has also been a serious student of our best poets. From the subject of his lean Ph.D. dissertation, *Such Holy Song: Music as Idea, Form and Image in the Poetry of William Blake,* Fairchild would glean a vision of "fearful symmetry," a notion that human making had or might have its parallel in the work of some "immortal hand or eye." Blake also educated Fairchild in versification. In the dissertation he notes those eighteenth-century prosodists who, opposing Samuel Johnson, argued for "a liberal prosody that helped to return English poetry to accentualism and opened the way to greater metrical variation." From Blake and from his more recent model, Anthony Hecht, Fairchild would learn about expanding the rhetoric of the poem, the cumulative power of the long sentence, the mixing of tones and levels of diction.

And let's not forget those other influences, just as important: the lore of baseball and jazz, rife with genius and failure, pop songs belted in the Bible Belt, and a fascination with French poetry, particularly the surrealists and their various offspring. *Local Knowledge* was first published in the *Quarterly Review of Literature* Poetry Series in 1991, and like so many books in those worthy groupings, it received too little notice. Due to his long-delayed but now undeniable success, Fairchild has been able to republish the book with Norton. His revisions are substantial and worth dwelling on. First and foremost, he has radically changed the sequence of poems so that readers will have a harder time lumping him among the regionalists and will have to grapple with his intellectual ambitions. The book now begins with "In Czechoslovakia," a big poem making use of the extraordinary Holocaust film *The Shop on Main Street,* and the poet's own experience during and after a viewing of the movie:

> and the world deepens without darkening and the faces
> of everyone are a kind of ovation, and then it's over,
> you think, the house lights go up, and you're sitting there
> stunned and the woman from the front row walks out
> into the aisle with her hand out behind her as if gripping
> another, smaller hand. And you see it, though
> you don't want to, because you are a man or a woman,
> you see that there is nothing there, no child,
> nothing, and the woman stops and bends down to speak
>
> to the child that isn't there and she has this smile
> of adulation, this lacemaker's gaze of contentment,
> *she is perfectly happy,* and she walks on out
> into the street where people are walking up and down
> and where you will have to walk up and down
> as if you were on a boulevard in Czechoslovakia
> watching that endless cortege of gray trucks
> rumble by in splendid alignment as you go on thinking
> and breathing as usual, wreathed in your own human skin.

This enlargement of sympathies—from film to deluded woman to an admission of one's own humanity—makes a much bolder opening to a very good book. The scene is both remembered and imagined, and the poet's ability to build rhetorical power in long sentences that carry the poem to the killer ending will become a hallmark of Fairchild's narratives.

I don't mean to slight other good poems in the book, such as "Language, Nonsense, Desire," "The Doppler Effect," his revised title sequence or his fine sestina, "There Is a Constant Movement in My Head." But Fairchild's revision repositions the regional poems of memory and ups the intellectual ante, if you will. The book now ends with "*L'Attente*," a poem in which "The little man sitting at the top of the stairs" could well be the mind itself, "waiting for the dancing to begin."

I'm not the only reader to call Fairchild a poet of mind. D. Z. Phillips did so in an essay for *Midwest Studies in Philosophy*. But the point is worth underscoring because some others have read him as if he were merely an aging professor sentimentalizing the physical life of work. Fairchild's best poems have to be read as shaped things, manufactured expertly from the materials of *mémagination*. The fact that he was so long unrecognized as an artist says more about the limits of contemporary publishing and criticism than it does about him. But you know the rest, or some of it, anyway. In 1998 Alice James Books brought out his third full-length collection, *The Art of the Lathe*, with a preface by Anthony Hecht, and the book swept so many awards that the poet's life would never be the same. In fact, I cannot remember another volume in recent decades that made such a big splash in the small pond of American poetry. When Fairchild performed its two anchoring masterpieces, "Body and Soul" and "Beauty," audiences felt carried away by an unaccustomed grandeur.

Much has already been said about these two marvelous poems. What I most want to emphasize is Fairchild's technique as a verse narrator. In the baseball poem "Body and Soul," the lines come perilously close to prose, but the arc of the story, the way you think it's going to end with its central revelation while Fairchild pushes through to an even more devastating finish, creates its own charge and elevation well above the minutiae of versification. "Beauty," of course, begins not in the Midwest machine shop but "at the Bargello in Florence," the poet and his wife gazing at Donatello's *David*. The poem's title word then unrolls a narrative, sustained by loose hexameters and commanding rhetoric, with surprising juxtapositions of high art and ordinary lives, about manhood, failures of connection, even the assassination of J.F.K.—but ultimately about the effort of the mind to apprehend experience in some tenable form, about beauty and the lack of it, mysteries we are immersed in "like the dyer's hand."

*The Art of the Lathe* is, like all of Fairchild's books, intelligently organized, the poems playing off each other like echoes in a deep well. The range of references is again eclectic and surprising: Georg Trakl, Patsy Cline, Heidegger, Leonardo, Diderot, Plumier, Oliver Sacks, Orson Welles, etc. The poet seems an intellectual packrat who can haul just the right quotation from the ravelings of his nest in order to set his language on edge, to give it an ironic or illuminating spin. The book's success led to somewhat greater freedom in his teaching life and a contract with Norton for a new collection, *Early Occult Memory Systems of the Lower Midwest,* which won the National Book Critics Circle Award and established Fairchild at last as a poet who really could not be dismissed.

That long title has put some readers off. I thought it was a mistake too, but on further reflection I see how it suits the author's bid to be taken seriously as a thinker. These occult memory systems are poems, of course, part of that connectivity and transformation of experience. But this time Fairchild has another philosopher up his sleeve, Ramon Lull, or "Doctor Illuminatus," a thirteenth-century poet, theologian and hermit. According to William Turner in the *Catholic Encyclopedia,* Lull "invented a mechanical contrivance, a logical machine, in which the subjects and predicates of theological propositions were arranged in circles, squares, triangles, and other geometrical figures, so that by moving a lever, turning a crank, or causing a wheel to revolve, the propositions would arrange themselves in the affirmative or negative and thus prove themselves to be true. This device he called the *Ars Generalis Ultima* or the *Ars Magna.*" Essentially, Lull wanted to make explicit the connection between theology and philosophy. His invention sounds a bit like Johnny Rebeck's sausage machine or a Rube Goldberg fantasy, and I suspect that Fairchild is both serious and whimsical when he alludes to it. His book is ordered analogously, but he seems less interested in proving absolutes than in hearing secret harmonies.

Once again we have strong narratives, including "Rave On" and "The Blue Buick." We have "The Memory Palace," a prose meditation built upon quotations from Agee. We have a number of well-wrought lyrics, such as the title poem with its meditations on word and world, and "Hearing Parker for the First Time," "On the Passing of Jesus Freaks from the College Classroom," "Weather Report," "The Second Annual *Wizard of Oz* Reunion in Liberal, Kansas," and "At Omaha Beach." We also have confirmation of a fact that seems to have eluded some of Fairchild's critics: he can be damned funny, as in "Brazil," his poem about "Elton Wayne Showalter, redneck surrealist," or "Luck," his riff on literary careers with its wry self-evaluation and play upon the "uck" sounds in English. In this book, too, Fairchild presents a range of characters, not only his family, but also Mrs. Hill, Moses Yellow Horse, Travis Doyle and Roy Garcia, a working-class poet who first appeared in *The Art of the Lathe.* Now we actually get three prose poems by Garcia following his appearance in "The Blue Buick," so Fairchild's aesthetic range expands—Pessoa-like—to take in other personae, influenced particularly by Rene Char. In fact, "The Blue Buick" begins with an epigraph from another French poet, Blaise Cendrars, about a reading experience "which turned me upside down and, in short, baptized me, or at the very least, converted me to Poetry, initiated me into the Word, catechized me."

Surely that passage is dear to B. H. Fairchild, whose baptism in life and art has been so variously fed, and whose accomplishment has been to hold and shape so much experience, so much memory and imagination. Take, for example, his narrative "Rave On," which builds to a near-suicidal climax as four young men set out to roll a car for the thrill of it. Just when you think Fairchild has found his ending, he pauses for breath and keeps on going:

> I survived. We all did. And then came the long surrender,
> the long, slow drifting down like young hawks riding on
> the purest, thinnest air, the very palm of God
> holding them aloft so close to something hidden there,
> and then the letting go, the fluttering descent, claws
> spread wide against the world, and we become, at last,
> our fathers. And do not know ourselves and therefore
> no longer know each other. Mike Luckinbill ran a Texaco
> in town for years. Billy Heinz survived a cruel divorce,
> remarried, then took to drink. But finally last week

I found this house in Arizona where the brothers
take new names and keep a vow of silence and make
a quiet place for any weary, or lost, passenger
of earth whose unquiet life has brought him there,
and so, after vespers, I sat across the table
from men who had not surrendered to the world,
and one of them looked at me and looked into me,
and I'm telling you there was *a fire in his head*
and his eyes were coming fast down a caliche road,
and I knew this man, and his name was Travis Doyle.

The very notion of surrendering to the world, like the bear
Wahb or like the men who cannot forgive a baseball genius who
shows up at their amateur game in "Body and Soul," is the crux
of Fairchild's vision of both life and art. Art is not a surrender.
It might not always be a victory, mind you, but it is not a surrender. It's as if all of Fairchild's work, narrative and lyric, were
about the mind moving upon silence, about our apprehension
of patterns and our terror that nothing underlies them. The
well-turned verbal object must open to the uncanny or it will
never hold experience, which is always just beyond our comprehension. A story is *mythistorema*, mythic and historical, and
when it is given rhythmic power and cast into lines that story res-
onates like music. I do not say it is music. I say it is like music,
and has to be felt or it cannot be understood. The poet's ambition is to stop time, if only for a moment, so that time can be
turned in the hand like a rounded stone, shaped as on a lathe
or in a river.

The end of Fairchild's longest narrative, "The Blue Buick," is
like this, charging recollection almost as James Joyce does at the
end of "The Dead":

I stood there a long time listening to the soft crush
of clumps of snow as they dropped onto the street and then,
in the background, hearing the night sounds of horns
far away and a lone shout somewhere close by
and watching the lights in the gleaming blue surface
from passing cars and from the stars and the moon
and from anywhere there was any light at all
as all things seen and unseen and all kingdoms
naked in the human heart rose toward the sky.

This is the sort of accomplishment, it seems to me, that earns Fairchild a place among our best contemporary poets. It was recognized as such by the late Anthony Hecht, which means a great deal to the man whose work this essay celebrates. Hecht was a master of pacing and insight, a poet of ambitious range and magisterial panache. Fairchild is very much his own man, but is reaching a Hechtian level. For a poet to have such immediacy, such command of the dramatic and narrative structures that will carry an audience to heightened awareness, both tragic and comic, for him to speak to people who may not love poetry as well as those who spend their lives studying it, does more to validate the art than anything a critic can say.

# The Limits of the
# Literary Movement

Modern poets differ from the Elizabethans in this.
Each of the moderns like an Elector of Hanover
governs his own petty state.
                                    —John Keats

. . . And when I am formulated, sprawling on a pin,
When I am pinned and wriggling on the wall,
Then how should I begin
To spit out all the butt-ends of my days and ways?
                                    —T. S. Eliot

All poetry is experimental poetry.
                    —Wallace Stevens

Literary movements are trumped up to make careers or make
life easier for professors, but they often become albatrosses
around the necks of the writers they were intended to elevate.
Modernism was not a single movement, yet the term is sometimes used to denote a unified revolutionary front of the sort
envisioned by Filippo Marinetti, who advocated destroying the
museums and was a big fan of the absolute. But many Modernists were obsessed with the past. Ezra Pound, one of the pa-
trons of modern free verse, had friendships with Yeats and Frost,
and admired Hardy. Movements associated with Modernism include Futurism, Vorticism and Imagism. Only the last of these
has had an enduring effect upon poetic practice. The Imagist
anthologies packed in poets practicing visual and minimalist
styles, yet they also contain writers as unlike each other as Eliot,
Lawrence and Joyce. In some cases, a writer's inclusion in an
Imagist anthology (whether made by Pound or by Amy Lowell)
feels as arbitrary as a lottery.

Even in an apparently cohesive group like Britain's Movement poets I can discern differences between Philip Larkin and Robert Conquest, Kingsley Amis and Thom Gunn. And what can I say of the Martians? Well, for one, I can say that the founder of that odd little movement, Craig Raine, is still alive and writing well in England, no doubt grumbling on occasion that he is remembered only for a single poem he published in the 1970s. Movements are like fads with traction. If they take, they take for a long time. Sooner or later someone gives them a name and begins to identify their characteristics. When the anthologies appear, the fight is on.

I raise this issue because, just the other day in a book review, I found myself writing of Language Poets as if they were all the same, as if one could find no essential differences between Lyn Hejinian, Michael Palmer and Ron Silliman. As it happens, Language Poets have been pretty clear in staking their critical ground, which might be called a kind of academic counter-culturalism, as much beholden to schools of literary theory as anything else. But even if they choose to toe a party line, the very act of lumping them all together in this way creates an inevitable injustice, and critics ought to be aware of what they are doing when they do it. The same can be said of New Formalism, a term used as if it defined a small coterie of clones. In his introduction to a very good anthology, *New British Poetry* (2004), the Scottish poet Don Paterson attempts to define a "Mainstream" poetry as distinct from a "Postmodern" one. But he wants to remove the British literary tradition in which his generation works from anything that smacks of "the clumping clog-dance of the New Formalists from the school of Yvor Winters onwards." It's a clever phrase, loaded with unspecified literary history, and I can think of several poets to whom it might be applied. But the influence of Yvor Winters, who reigned so long at Stanford, also extends to Thom Gunn, Donald Hall, Robert Pinsky, and a variety of other poets.

You see my point. Our critical shorthand, the very categories in which many of us participate for our own benefit, becomes inaccurate as a method of evaluation. I say this as a poet and editor sometimes associated with New Formalism. Maybe it's time to let the term wither away. As it happens, I have always disparaged it in private and in print, largely because I mistrust claims of novelty and believe that formalist designs are insufficient markers of any art. When I reviewed a book of essays in Expansive Poetry (another common term for New Formalism) in the *Georgia Review* (Winter 1990), I said that the title sounded like a balloon about to burst. What underlay my comment was partly an anxiety about being too easily pegged as any sort of poet. While it is true that I have encountered editors hostile to rhyme and meter—and even one who advised me to avoid rich sound effects like alliteration—it is also true that I wanted to be free to attempt any poetic form available, from free verse to the verse novel. I wanted something unrealistic: not to be condemned for what I love. My model in formal terms was a protean figure like Auden, though I wanted an earthier sense of peoples' lives in what I wrote. More than anything else, I did not want to fall into the too-common rut of self-parody by writing only one kind of poetry. Over time, of course, one learns one has limits; one does some things well and not others. But saying so is very different from lumping poets into classes and categories.

Like every other writer who has indulged in criticism, I must occasionally eat my words. Still, I find that a number of the concerns stated by New Formalist poets and critics had validity when they were stated. There *was* a complacency about poetic form in contemporary poetry criticism. There *were* critics who associated a poet's formal choices with political ones, forgetting that Pound was a fascist while many leftists wrote in rhyme and meter (Auden, Neruda and Thomas McGrath come readily to mind). When, more than a decade ago, I co-edited (with Mark Jarman) a controversial anthology, *Rebel Angels: 25 Poets of the New Formalism*, I hoped we would make a case for the viability of certain poetic techniques among younger writers. The book sold well, was reprinted and received dozens of reviews all over the globe ranging from howls of protest and indignant denunciations to lavish praise. What struck me most about the reviews, both pro and con, was how inaccurate they were, as if the book's polemical nature had reduced all the poetry it contained to cannon (or should I say canon?) fodder.

No doubt Mark and I made some mistakes in editing the book, but most of the twenty-five writers we included still have productive, even innovative careers. These include Elizabeth Alexander, Rafael Campo, Dana Gioia, Emily Grosholz, R. S. Gwynn, Marilyn Hacker, Rachel Hadas, Andrew Hudgins, Sydney Lea, Brad Leithauser, Phillis Levin, Charles Martin, Wyatt Prunty, Rachel Wetzteon and Greg Williamson—not a clog dancer in the lot. Our mistakes may have been to include so few poets and an insufficient formal variety. Having left so many out, we felt obliged to leave ourselves out as well.

Of course all anthologies are failures of one sort or another—too inclusive, too exclusive, too polemical, not polemical enough. In some way ours contributed to arguments about legitimacy in poetic practice. It was a small protest against those who would outlaw any sort of technique, because in poetry no technique can really ever be out of bounds. You have to look at the specific example and determine whether it works or not. Where our poets were faulted on technical grounds, the cases made were sometimes fair. But arguments labeling these poets as retrograde or conservative were hysterical in more ways than one. The notion that any art progresses in a straight line through technical innovation, abandoning the old, can be taken too far, as Eliot and Pound knew very well. We think we have progressed beyond the old, only to discover that some ancient human impulses are still very much with us.

One of these is storytelling. Nowadays some critics run around proclaiming that narrative is dead, or at least uninteresting, but must we believe what they say? What explains the perennial popularity of new translations of the classics? And what explains the vitality of narrative among contemporary poets as varied as B. H. Fairchild and Anne Carson? A poetics built on *thou shalt nots* (thou shalt not rhyme, thou shalt not commit a story, etc.) is an occasion to rebel. We must winnow the good from the bad, but we cannot do so without questioning all assumptions about technique, genre, diction and school.

Very well, then. New Formalism never became academically respectable, but it has had some impact on the scene in spite of this. I wince when the term gets used to cudgel poets I admire, just as I used to wince when it was used to curry favor. Reviewing A. E. Stallings's eloquent collection *Hapax* (2006), Peter Campion took the opportunity to fire a rather typical broadside, referring to New Formalism's "silly polemic against Modernism" (*Poetry*, January 2007). But has Stallings herself ever said anything against Modernism? And is there a single Modernism to oppose? Is it the Modernism of Marinetti? Pound? Frost? Auden? Seferis? Which New Formalists are intended? Charles Martin, with his classical training and deep understanding of the Black Mountain Poets? Dana Gioia, with his translations of such figures as Montale? Mark Jarman, so indebted to Jeffers? B. H. Fairchild, who adapted the elevated rhetoric of Anthony Hecht to his moving narratives? Perhaps Campion means, although he will not say it, the scholarly case made in Timothy Steele's *Missing Measures: Modern Poetry and the Revolt Against Meter* (1990). But Steele's argument is worth considering, assuming you can read the book with an open mind. Campion never specifies which New Formalists have driven him to such dismissals. The identification of the literary movement makes his job too easy, inviting smugness instead of criticism. I'm being hard on Campion, who after all was only writing a book review, but he was hard on poets he does not name.

I find Stallings a remarkable poet, partly for her ability to balance thought and emotion gracefully. Here is "Last Will," one of several moving poems about her father's death:

> What he *really* wanted, she confesses,
> Was to be funneled into shells and shot
> Across a dove field. Only, she could not—
>
> The kick of shotguns knocks her over. Well,
> I say, he'd understand. It doesn't matter
> What becomes of atoms, how they scatter.
>
> The priest reads the committal, something short.
> We drop the little velvet pouch of dust
> Down a cylindrical hole bored in the clay—
>
> And one by one, the doves descend, ash-gray,
> Softly as cinders on the parking lot,
> And silence sounds its deafening report.

Another I could cite on the same subject is her sonnet "*Sine Qua Non.*" Or I could mention the way she refreshes classical allusion in a poem like "First Love: A Quiz," written in the form of a multiple choice exam. I might never have encountered Stallings's fine work if the New Formalism hadn't happened, both because the climate of receptiveness to such poetry might not have occurred and because the West Chester Poetry Conference, where I first met her, might not have got off the ground and flourished.

Held each June in Pennsylvania, this large and lively gathering is associated in many peoples' minds with New Formalism, yet it has fostered the careers of writers like H. L. Hix, Kay Ryan, Bill Coyle and Chelsea Rathburn—writers it is not easy to pigeonhole. It was at West Chester that I met a poet I consider among the very best of my generation, the late Michael Donaghy, a Bronx native who held three passports: American, British and Irish. Michael was the single best poetry performer I have ever heard, an irreverent master. When he died suddenly in London at age fifty, the British press eulogized him in a manner few American poets will ever see. The fact that this vital American poet is so little known in his native country is a disgrace, and I put it down to our parochialism, our unwillingness to read widely with discernment, our herd mentality and lazy habits of criticism. Michael was a poet who could play the whole instrument without feeling hamstrung by critics and schools.

I will offer just two of his shorter poems in full. The first, "Machines," can now be found in *Collected Poems* (Picador, 2009):

> Dearest, note how these two are alike:
> This harpsichord pavane by Purcell
> And the racer's twelve-speed bike.
>
> The machinery of grace is always simple.
> This chrome trapezoid, one wheel connected
> To another of concentric gears,
> Which Ptolemy dreamt of and Schwinn perfected,
> Is gone. The cyclist, not the cycle, steers.
> And in the playing, Purcell's chords are played away.
>
> So this talk, or touch if I were there,
> Should work its effortless gadgetry of love,
> Like Dante's heaven, and melt into the air.

If it doesn't, of course, I've fallen. So much is chance,
So much agility, desire, and feverish care,
As bicyclists and harpsichordists prove

Who only by moving can balance,
Only by balancing move.

Notice the insouciance, the fresh conceit, the undergirding of authority in the lines. The poem is contemporary while delighting in what remains of the past.

Now in Michael's comic vein, here is "Local 32B." The title refers to the "US National Union of Building Service Workers," and the poem arose from Michael's high school job as a doorman in Manhattan.

The rich are different. Where we have doorknobs,
they have doormen—like me, a cigar store Indian
on the Upper East Side, in polyester, in August.
As the tenants tanned in Tenerife and Monaco
I stood guard beneath Manhattan's leaden light
watching poodle turds bake grey in half an hour.
*Another hot one, Mr. Rockefeller!*
An Irish doorman foresees his death,
waves, and runs to help it with its packages.
Once I got a cab for Pavarotti. No kidding.
No tip either. I stared after him down Fifth
and caught him looking after me, then through me,
like Samson, eyeless, at the Philistine chorus—
Yessir, I put the tenor in the vehicle.
And a mighty tight squeeze it was.

If I had space I could quote more profoundly moving poems by Michael, among them "The Tuning," in which he seems to predict his own early death, or "Remembering Steps to Dances Learned Last Night," where he riffs on Homer, Cavafy and Pound. I use these shorter poems to demonstrate how lightly he wore the mantle of mastery.

Michael had written a mixed review of *Rebel Angels* for a British periodical, but he came to West Chester and had a good time performing, teaching and talking. He liked the way the conference celebrated older writers (Hecht, Wilbur, Justice, Louis Simpson, Anne Stevenson and others) and tried to introduce British poets to American readers. As a four-day party for poetry, it has grown beyond the confines of a single literary movement. By the same token, all those concerns that once seemed so dire for New Formalists have been absorbed into contemporary poetic discourse. It's no longer difficult for young poets to seek out material on poetic forms, and in some cases editors are willing to publish work that makes use of such knowledge. New Formalism does not need to be flouted anymore, nor does it require defending. We can assume that any poetic technique is valid, so long as it is mastered.

What are literary movements for? They get writers noticed, sometimes for the wrong reasons. They make it easy for reviewers to lump named or unnamed individuals together, gesticulating broadly. They make for a tidy syllabus. But in the end they have precious little to do with poetry. The art of using language to its utmost has so many gradations of effect, so many technical choices, that it cannot be prejudged. To understand it we need readers of discernment who are willing to take poets and poems one at a time, readers who can admit the limitations of taste. Anthologies and reviews—and even movements—are a beginning, not an end.

# The Dhow's Gaze

## *Some Thoughts on Postcolonial Studies*

Oh East is East, and West is West, and never the twain shall
    meet,
Till Earth and Sky stand presently at God's great Judgment
    Seat;
But there is neither East nor West, Border, nor Bread, nor
    Birth,
When two strong men stand face to face, though they come
    from the ends of the Earth!
        —Rudyard Kipling

            Turn now and mourn
    That your existence is so deeply torn!
        —Farid ud-Din Attar, translated by
        Dick Davis and Afkham Darbandi

The world is not a text, although it is textured with texts.
    —Balachandra Rajan

I grew up in Washington State, a part of America rich in cultural and economic ties to Asia. My father modeled our yard on Japanese gardens he had seen, planting bamboo and maples that still thrive, building a curved bridge over a small gully beside our house. He and my mother hung Japanese scroll paintings on our walls. I doubt there was much depth to my family's understanding of such things, only an intuition that our landscape of misty hills and waterways was suited to these images from across the Pacific. We were, you might say, appropriating bits of a culture that we did not fully understand.

One year my father bought a small trailer for hauling our sailboat between Lake Whatcom and the Puget Sound. The man who sold him the trailer insisted that he also take a Pakistani dhow along with it, and my father happily obliged him. For much of our childhood, my brothers and I played on this dark teak hull, dramatically curved, with wooden fins on its stern and painted, forward-looking eyes on the prow. I recall that the boat was built as a gift for an American who had saved some peoples' lives in East Pakistan (now Bangladesh). It was certainly an extraordinary gift, beautifully constructed, with brass pins for the oars, every plank cut by hand. One year it became a float in a Bellingham parade. Several local children, including my younger brother and I, were dressed in costumes out of some Hollywood fantasy of the East, with turbans and painted beards. A local farmer, similarly garbed, drove his team of oxen that pulled the trailered dhow through the streets. A girl dressed in veils sat in the stern while we fanned her with fronds of some sort. We had stepped the mast, and it accidentally struck a stoplight we were passing under, scattering bits of colored glass down on us. We were surely the oddest float in the spring parade, but we succeeded in drawing attention to a fundraising effort for the local museum.

Once or twice we took the dhow out on the lake for a sail. We had not allowed its hull to swell in the water long enough, so it leaked dangerously and was hard to manage. But there it was, curved like a Persian slipper, bobbing in the waves of an American lake, its discolored sail bellied with wind. And the eyes of the dhow stared constantly ahead. I think now of how far those eyes had traveled, how strange the evergreen hills would have seemed if the eyes could really see. As strange and marvelous as the dhow appeared to us when we played pirates on its deck.

Years later the dhow decorated a Seattle restaurant for a while, and then my father donated it in memory of my older brother to the Center for Wooden Boats, where, a bit weathered, it can still be seen on display. "Chittagong Delta Boat," the sign says, "built around 1963 near Chittagong Delta between Pakistan and Burma." The hull planks have dried and shriveled, pulling apart, but someone has repainted the eyes.

જ

I begin with the dhow because it is an artifact of Asia imperfectly understood by Westerners. It reminds me of ways in which East and West meet each other's gaze with real difference, but it also makes me wonder about such differences. Even those distinctions—East, West, Europe, Asia, America—are simplifications of experience that hardly seem workable, especially in the evolving Global Village. Cultural difference is real enough, but so are the traits all human beings have in common. Just because some of our experience is culturally determined does not mean *all* of our experience is. In the twentieth century we have developed philosophies of difference, the Other, that have proved helpful in describing identity, gender politics, etc. In the academic field known as postcolonial studies (generally dealing with cultures after the withdrawal of European empires) we have—to borrow a phrase from the brilliant Indian writer O. V. Vijayan—"the theology of the difference." We hold our profound skepticism concerning human universals almost religiously. In particular, we massage the deep resentment and guilt produced by colonialism itself, the conviction that corrupting powers of colonizers have warped the societies of the colonized, that cultural misunderstanding is a crime unique to these imperialists and colonizers.

But postcolonial literature of the last fifty years or so demonstrates that misunderstanding, cultural or otherwise, is a human universal. Following Edward Said, many critics have read Western literature in terms of its misunderstandings of, or silence about, colonized peoples. But the colonized have also gazed at their colonizers with incomprehension, like those characters in Vijayan's story "Pedal Machine," who believe that "the white man had a pink face, like Gauranga the monkey god, and it was but a reasonable supposition that he must have a tail hidden within his tubular apparel." Vijayan's book of stories *After the Hanging* (Penguin, 1989) might best be described as "Kafka meets the Bhagavad-Gita." Written in Malayalam and translated into English by their author, these stories display a Hindu ecumenism; they cast a disillusioned eye both east and west. One can't always tell whether Vijayan responds to the world with religious humility or cold pessimism, and because of this ambiguity the stories seem situated precisely in our moment, so rich and confusing in its cultural impurity.

I feel the same way about R. K. Narayan, who is too often dismissed for his simplicity as a storyteller. A novel like his *The*

*Painter of Signs* (Penguin, 1977) pulls us into these modern dilemmas in ways that are gently disturbing and not at all simplistic. In it, a young man, Raman, lives with his aunt, who appears quaintly traditional in her observance of Hindu rituals. Raman thinks of himself as an enlightened, "modern" man, fills his room with English books and mocks the superstitious behavior of his townspeople. Yet Raman is just as superstitious and irrational in his own way. He is obsessed with appearances. After all, he paints *signs*. Whether Narayan studied semiology I do not know; I suspect that his knowledge of signification derives instead from Hindu tradition, particularly the concept of *maya*.

Raman falls in love with Daisy, an Indian woman who has taken on Western ways, not only in her choice of a name but also in her missionary zeal for birth control. This is Narayan's critique of Indira Gandhi's emergency measures of the 1970s, when the government went so far as to sterilize a great many peasants in the Indian countryside. Suddenly we see that Raman is a kind of Everyman, pulled between the tradition of the aunt and the modernity of Daisy. But it is not so simple. We cannot tell whether Daisy's work to limit population growth is a denial of her *dharma* (sacred duty) as a woman, or is a part of God's plan. We cannot say whether the aunt's ablutions and sacrifices are made out of genuine piety or a misguided martyrdom. Poor Raman, the deluded protagonist, is in love with illusions. Daisy may or may not love him in return. These characters are caught—as I would argue all of us are caught—in a tar pit of conflicting traditions, beliefs, demands and possibilities. East and West are part of it. Male and Female are part of it. And so are Science and Religion, Society versus the Individual—just about any dialectical arrangement you can name. For both Vijayan and Narayan, I suspect, this muddle could be the very definition of human experience, and our postcolonial era has only given that experience a particular flavor without fundamentally altering it.

Asian writers have looked at the West as long as Western writers have looked at Asia. The twelfth-century Sufi poet Farid ud-Din Attar tells a story of Sheikh Sam'an, who falls in love with a Christian girl, travels with her to Rome and renounces his own faith. This is from *The Conference of the Birds*, in Dick Davis and Afkham Darbandi's fluid translation:

Love sacked his heart; the girl's bewitching hair
Twined round his faith impiety's smooth snare.
The sheikh exchanged religion's wealth for shame,
A hopeless heart submitted to love's fame.
"I have no faith," he cried. "The heart I gave
Is useless now; I am the Christian's slave."

The sheikh commits all sorts of sins, even drinking wine:

The old wine sidled through the old man's veins
And like a twisting compass turned his brains;
Old wine, young love, a lover far too old,
Her soft arms welcoming—could he be cold?

But the Sufi text views such sin as an unavoidable part of the Way, the path to God, rather than a reason for sending the sheikh to hell. If conversion is seduction and Christianity associated (oddly enough) with sexual wiles, the sheikh still has a friend in Mecca who will bring him home—the true friend, the Prophet. When the sheikh repents and receives purification, the Christian girl follows him, again out of desire for "the Other." She converts to his faith, but like a fish out of water she cannot survive in its atmosphere. This Sufi parable about the attractions and dangers of conversion becomes deeply compassionate, condemning neither character while understanding the nature of their differences.

Whoever knows love's path is soon aware
That stories such as this are far from rare.
All things are possible, and you may meet
Despair, forgiveness, certainty, deceit.
The Self ignores the secrets of the Way,
The Mysteries no mortal speech can say;
Assurance whispers in the heart's dark core,
Not in the muddied Self—a bitter war
Must rage between these two. Turn now and mourn
That your existence is so deeply torn!

We can find narratives of conversion in the West too, in writers like Boccaccio. East and West have been gazing at each other, using each other as images of Otherness, for a long time.

Translations like Davis and Darbandi's allow us an understanding, however imperfect, of specific cultures. But we should also remember that colonialism and commerce have made English a global force, and that one of the questions many writers in postcolonial societies must ask is what language they will write in. What language should a Lakota writer use? A Nigerian? An Irish? A Scot? A Chicano or Chicana? A Pakistani? An Indian? The fact that English is not only used but enriched by writers all over the world is significant, as is the fact that other writers—sometimes in defiance of the marketplace—insist upon traditional tongues. Writers from the Indian subcontinent who use English—Salman Rushdie, Bapsi Sidhwa, R. K. Narayan, Vikram Seth, et al.—are more likely to achieve success in the global marketplace than writers like Sunil Gangopadhyay, O. V. Vijayan and the late Faiz Ahmed Faiz, who are known outside their homelands only through translations. But perhaps translation also becomes a metaphor for all intercultural reading. Issues of language and identity are deeply rooted—the evolution of English in *England,* let alone in other parts of the world, is fraught with conflict. Arguments for cultural purity, whether from the left or the right, now seem more dated and distasteful than ever, yet one cannot always shrug off one's cultural identity in favor of some pluralistic ideal. Think of the territorial war between India and Pakistan. Think of Yugoslavia or the Middle East. These animosities, it would seem, cannot be wished away. The eyes of the dhow gaze on a world that is deeply torn.

≈

At its best, postcolonial studies accomplishes two things: it complicates history by asking us to say more than "Alas" to the defeated, and it complicates literary study by presenting challenges to the Western canon. Nothing wrong with that. Canons are always (and always have been) arguable. I have Edward Said to thank for introducing me to a haunting Sudanese novel, Tayeb Salih's *Season of Migration to the North* (translated by Denys Johnson-Davies), which I have taught in literature classes for several years. Salih's novel is precisely about the East-West gaze I have been describing, and how cultural collisions have made "hollow men" of many people in the modern world. It is about the necessity of stories and those elements of identity that stand between us and madness. Once I had a Saudi student who read the book in my class. He came into my office, clutching the book to his heart, and said, "This book is *me!*" The more you know of the book, the more disturbed you will be by this confession, yet I don't think the experience it describes is entirely unavailable to sympathetic Western readers. Narrative is one place where strangers can meet and recognize each other.

Still, literary knowledge and sympathy are not really the same as intimate cultural knowledge, especially when one does not know the language of the author one is reading in translation. One of the weaknesses of postcolonial studies is the illusion it creates that we can have a profound knowledge of historical and political issues by reading only literature and criticism. Another perhaps related weakness is the implication that all history and politics are relative. Balachandra Rajan's scholarly study *Under Western Eyes: India from Milton to Macaulay* (1998) is an ambitious attempt to address not only the literary history of its title, but also the academic discipline of postcolonial studies. The book's strengths are many, including its author's deep learning in multiple traditions—he is Emeritus Professor of English at the University of Western Ontario, and his books include *The Form of the Unfinished: English Poetics from Spenser to Pound* (1985), as well as two novels. Rajan can think like a novelist, a historical critic and a theorist.

From my point of view, this complex of talents also makes his book frustrating to read. His subject is a great one, full of eccentric characters like Elihu Yale, who made a fortune in India during the seventeenth century. "To the university that bears his name," Professor Rajan writes, "he left the sum of £500, two trunks of textiles, and 417 books." There is also the Portuguese adventurer and poet Luís Vaz de Camões, author of "*The Lusiads,* his poem celebrating Vasco de Gama's passage to India." The latter becomes, for Rajan, a kind of propagandist for Portuguese business interests. There are Milton and Dryden, Hegel, Shelley and Macaulay, most of them, according to Rajan, complicit in Europe's (particularly England's) misreading of India, therefore sharing in the guilt of Empire. Yet, as an imaginative author, Rajan knows that "to write a poem is to transgress ideologies."

Real literature is too complex for mere ideology, too confounded by its own contradictions and ambiguities. This understanding, as well as the great stories he has to tell, makes the book worth reading.

But there is also a Mr. Hyde to this Dr. Jekyll, an academic who murders lucidity every time he faces an audience of professors. The book evolved not only out of its author's research, but at academic conferences, where no doubt he was told he had to say something about every critic who has ever contributed to the field. Some of this is good, such as his introduction's respectful but firm dismissal of Edward Said's simplifications in *Orientalism*. But the culture of the academic conference has also caused Rajan to forget his own strengths as a writer. Whenever he proves he has read the required critics, his prose becomes both clotted and abstract. Here is Rajan as Dr. Jekyll:

> Imperialisms obviously vary, although in spotlighting their differences one should remember the quip to which Krishna Menon was addicted: to ask a subject people which imperialism they prefer is like asking a fish whether it would rather be fried in margarine or butter.

And here is Mr. Hyde:

> An independence struggle within the self must somehow discover a rhetoric that reconciles its own decolonization with the aims of an empire it seeks beyond itself.

I could translate that sentence for you, but I shouldn't have to. The sad thing about this book is that its important arguments will be read only by other professors who will translate them into the same abstractions and publish them in books that will be read by still more professors if they are read at all. Postcolonial studies supposes that literature does have some relationship to the world beyond the university, but prose like this insists that such a world can't possibly give a damn.

The moment he steps out of his introduction, however, Rajan becomes a better writer. This is not to say there are no more lapses into pure abstraction, but that he does have stories to tell and facts to relay. For example, Camões's *The Lusiads* may well have been an epic of imperial commerce, but its historical effect was its contribution to the destruction of Portugal as a world power:

> Portugal's declining fortunes became catastrophically evident when King Sebastiao in June 1578 led an expedition to Alcácer-Kebir to verify Camões's assurance that the Moslem everywhere would quail in terror before the weight of Portugal's armies and the fame of its exploits. The king had reasons for confidence apart from Camões's poetry. Fifty years earlier, in celebration of a triumph by the Portuguese over the Moors, a subservient Moor had ridden a lavishly caparisoned white elephant, curtseying thrice before the pope and sprinkling the assembled spectators with water. On this occasion, the outcome would be different, even with an invading force of 1,500 horsemen and 15,000 foot soldiers, transported by 500 vessels. Nine thousand camp followers accompanied the expedition, including large numbers of women, to celebrate the victory in the manner of canto 9 of *The Lusiads*. In four hours of battle under a searing African sun, the flower of Portugal's manhood was destroyed. Eight thousand were killed, and 15,000 taken prisoner and sold into slavery. No more than 100 found their way to safety. In the following year, as the plague descended on Lisbon, Camões contracted his final illness, commenting that he was glad to die not merely in but also with his country.

Who says poetry makes nothing happen? It's Rajan's command of historical and literary detail, and his understanding of the dangers in confusing the two, that made me unwilling to stop reading. As a writer, Camões condescended to Moslems and Hindus, and by doing so he demonstrably contributed to imperial suicide.

Rajan's story, then, is about European awareness of India, and how the rhetoric of literary artists, philosophers and historians contributed to or struggled against that of institutions like the British East India Company. In the case of a literary genius like Milton, India plays a complicated role. Milton certainly knew of the wealth and greatness of the Mughal Empire: "When *Paradise Lost* was published, the monarch on the Peacock Throne was Dryden's hero, Aurangzeb. He could be said to have been raised to his eminence by merit, if by merit we mean the successful killing off of every other claimant." Both Milton and Dryden used the Mughals for images of exotic wealth. Both seem to have been naively unaware that Indian history could be as bloody as that of the English. Milton was, of course, a revolutionary, and Rajan suggests that he equated Satan with the colonizers of distant lands. Yet Milton's position was also contradictory. He supported the rebel Cromwell, who became the tyrant Cromwell, ransacking Ireland and persecuting many of his own people. Milton surely enjoyed Satan's rebelliousness as a literary creation, but that doesn't mean he would have associated Beelzebub with his boss. The same Milton who seems to have averted his eyes from Cromwell's crimes created in his epics a convincing critique of empire. Milton seems to associate India with the infernal, the Tartar with Tartarus, but also to criticize that association by the manner in which Satan "colonizes" a world resembling the Orient. Rajan does not mention Blake's statement that Milton was secretly of the Devil's party, but he does assert that even *Paradise Lost* cannot subvert the Empire's "geography of privilege."

I can see Milton's failings as a revolutionary here, his complicity with empire even as he criticizes it, but I also wonder if Rajan isn't using one of the postcolonial assumptions we should continue to question. Our egalitarian ideals make it difficult to raise such questions, but let me try: Is there any conquered people that has not also been at some time a conquerer? I certainly see the injustice of colonial power, but I wonder if colonial power is not one of the symptoms of evil rather than its cause. As I read this book, I was also reading about the crisis in Yugoslavia, where, to use Auden's lines, "Those to whom evil is done / Do evil in return." Human cruelty and misunderstanding are universal attributes. All religions call upon our better natures, but literature and history are full of our failure to achieve such ideals.

Seeing the infernal in India would become more common in the nineteenth century. But that is not the only kind of misreading that Rajan objects to. There is also the example of Dryden's drama *Aureng-Zebe,* in which the murderous Moghul emperor becomes "the new model of the Restoration hero, triumphant through moderation rather than destroyed by excess, combining patience with the capacity to act decisively, able to stand and wait but also able to seize the day, but only in the interests of the nation." On the contrary, Rajan says, "Jacobean tragedy is the proper genre of Mughul history." Ultimately, Dryden's appropriation and misuse of Indian history strike Rajan as a sign of disrespect "that no writer would have thought of bringing to bear on the Greek and Roman past. Such disrespect points to a stubbornly resident devaluation of the Orient." He is probably right in this extreme case—though Shakespeare misused English history to suit his own ends, and I do wonder just how far we can take the argument for historical accuracy in literature. A great deal of imaginative literature, as Professor Rajan knows, involves the appropriation of someone else's experience, and we are left weighing that injustice against the transformative powers of the writer in question.

Not all of the English were as negative toward India as Oliver Goldsmith, who called Indians "a feeble race of sensualists, too dull to find rapture in any pleasures and too indolent to turn their gravity into wisdom." If there is a hero in Rajan's narrative, it might be William Jones, a scholar who founded the Asiatic Society of Bengal in the 1770s. While much British policy denigrated Hindu in favor of Moslem India, Jones saw Hinduism as "central rather than marginal and even as a cornerstone of the edifice of civilization or a lost chapter of the Western identity. Sanskrit was a parent language of humankind, and Sanskrit philosophy and literature were distinguished statements in the history of civilization." Such propositions seem self-evident to many of us now, but the story Rajan tells concerns the relative neglect of Jones's ideas in favor of James Mill's *A History of British India,* which became "standard reading for officials of the East India Company," even though its author "never visited India and made no attempt to interest himself in any of its languages." Again, imperial arrogance too often excuses ignorance about an empire's subject peoples. The same British Empire would produce sympathetic eccentrics like William Jones, Edward Fitzgerald, Richard Burton and T. E. Lawrence, but these figures rarely wielded significant power in the Empire's actual workings, which were commercial and increasingly racist.

The most openly racist of the European intellectuals discussed by Rajan is Georg Wilhelm Friedrich Hegel, who saw skin color (the paler the better) as a correlative of enlightenment. Rajan argues that in fact Hegel's philosophy owes something to the same Hinduism that the philosopher denigrated on racial grounds. He goes on to discuss views of India in the work of two women writers, Elizabeth Hamilton and Lady Morgan (Sydney Owenson), reminding us that castes and poojahs existed in England too. In Robert Southey he finds another misinformed denunciation of Hinduism, whereas in Percy Bysshe Shelley he at least admires the elevation of Promethean over Christian heroism. Rajan approves of Shelley's "awareness of the constitutive power of language," but I wonder if this doesn't send him off into theoretical La-La Land. Remember, Shelley called poets "the unacknowledged legislators of the world"—English departments these days would substitute critics for poets, but they would still be wrong. And Rajan also has to admit that Shelley looked down his nose at the reality of India. Asia worked for him only as a symbol.

Macaulay and Marx are the next writers who erroneously assume British superiority in Rajan's narrative, and from this "long history of misrepresentation" he at last turns to another question: How might India wish to see itself? The image he prefers is that of Draupadi, who in the Mahabharata was joined to all of the Pandava brothers. "Draupadi can be humiliated but not disrobed; the legend not merely preserved in the pages of the world's longest epic but also celebrated in song and dance everywhere in India is tenacious in its hold on the imagination." Earlier in the book, Rajan admits that India's record in terms of the abuse of women is not so hot, even though Hindu culture exalts the feminine in many ways. Our cultural ideals often have little to do with our actual behavior. This, I would argue, is another universal truth.

"India and the West are enormous simplifications," Rajan writes, "and one cannot be deaf to the irony of using the homogenizing language of imperialism to mark out a terrain for the distinctive postcolonial gathering of voices. If the irony is not to become an embarrassment, we need to admit that major coalescences of diversity such as 'India,' with a long and stubborn history of self-imagining, have a place that is vital in the tissue of cultural thought."

Yes, and we should also admit the limits of cultural thought or of literary study as a measure of the world. But that shouldn't prevent us from reading each other, face to face or from a great distance, trying to get it right.

# Close to Seferis

In essence the poet has one theme: his live body.
—George Seferis, *A Poet's Journal,*
translated by Athan Anagnostopoulos

The first Greek to win the Nobel Prize for literature, George Seferis is still not as well understood or highly regarded as he deserves to be. He was quietly heroic in both art and life, a modern literary Odysseus, a poet of *nóstos* spilling into nostalgia, but never sentimental. His wounds, both personal and public, made him a kind of representative man in the way Emerson said all poets are. A rigorous and innovative writer, Seferis was also a servant of reason in turbulent times, often abused for his refusal to betray his principles. Among English readers he is usually compared to T. S. Eliot, but this comparison is wide of the mark. Seferis was a poet of greater sensuality and worldly experience than Eliot, and one finds no trace in his poems of the anti-Semitism that marred the American's work.

The only reason Seferis is not as widely known and studied as Eliot is that he wrote in Greek, a language spoken by some fifteen million people globally, not all of whom, it is safe to say, read poetry. Many Greek speakers, however, have *sung* Seferis. Several of his poems were set to music by Mikis Theodorakis, the leftist composer. Once in an outdoor café in Athens during a bibulous conversation, I sang a few bars of Seferis's "Epiphany, 1937" to a Syrian Greek who had tried to describe his sense of exile, and in response this fellow nudged his cousin, saying, "He knows. He knows what our life is like." But it was Seferis who knew, a poet of continuity and loss, of the private self in revolt against mediocrity and horror. He was a difficult poet, to be sure, but the popularity of a few of his poems attests to moments of feeling that could touch virtually anyone.

There are ideas aplenty in these poems; there are complexities of style, allusions, feints, even secrets. But in spite of their disillusionment, at times their bitterness, the poems are a pleasure to read, ranging widely in their tones and flavors. Often they seem to speak the Aegean into being. Writing about his poem entitled *Thrush*, Seferis admitted to "a very organic feeling that identifies humaneness with the Greek landscape." And indeed, despite a bloody history, there is something about the climate, the near-proverbial light, the contained variety of topography, the sea and the continuity of language from Homer to the present day that strike many people in the same way. Some poets are born of language, others are born of language and place, a sort of mutual saturation of word and experience. Seferis is the latter kind of poet. But it's not only his technique and absorption of important influences that make him a great poet; it's also his moment (1900–1971) and his ability to speak of its traumas and attractions. Good translations have been made of his work, but even his ablest translators would admit that much is lost of its aural wealth.[1]

When he published his first collection, *Strophé* (meaning both "stanza" and "turning point"), in 1931, Seferis decorated the title page with his drawing of the Gorgóna, a mermaid with two tails curving upward toward either side of her head. In Greek folklore the sister of Alexander the Great had been transformed into this vengeful creature. If a fisherman caught her in his net she would challenge him with a question: "Where is Alexander the Great?" The poor fisherman had to answer properly—"Alexander the Great lives and reigns"—or the Gorgóna would swamp his boat and send him to Davy Jones.

It is hard for us to imagine a culture in which obeisance must be paid to a short-lived emperor two millennia past, but this folktale illustrates the irredentist dreams of modern Greece. After the decline of Hellenism, the conquest of Rome and the braided culture of Byzantium, after four hundred years of humiliating rule by the Ottomans, the nation that emerged from the War of Independence in the 1820s possessed very little of the land once considered "Greek"—really just the tip of the Balkan peninsula and an island or two. Like all European nations at the dawn of modern nationalism, Greece was not even sure of its language, and Greeks experimented with both a synthetic "purified" tongue and demotic speech. Greek poets of the nineteenth century staked linguistic claims of one sort or another, just as the fledgling nation with its imported Bavarian king and competing politicians sought more of the ancient territory. This anxiety over culture and national borders resulted in the "Great Idea," a sort of Manifest Destiny concerning a greater Greece—not such a great idea when you consider the geopolitical changes wrought in the last two thousand years.

Among the political forces competing for power in modern Greece we find the monarchists, the republicans who would unite under the Cretan Eleftherios Venizelos, and the militarists who stepped in to control things whenever the first two factions lost their grip. It is important to know that Seferis grew up in a Venizelist household, steeped in the romance of a territorially completed Greece. Yet he was born a second-class citizen of the Ottoman Empire in Smyrna, and his early consciousness would have been formed by the impression that much of what he loved, including the land of Niobe and Anaxagoras, existed under the Sultan's rule.

Such ancient and troubled identity obsessed the poet all his life. In 1963, the day after accepting the Nobel Prize in Stockholm, Seferis delivered a lecture in which he ruminated upon the dilemma of neo-Hellenism: "I shall not say that we are of the same blood [as the ancients]—because I have a horror of racial theories—but we still live in the same country and we see the same mountains ending in the sea" (trans. Roderick Beaton). Like all legacies, Greek identity could be burdensome, and part of the burden was its uncertainty. After all, a modern Turkish counterpart, the poet Nazim Hikmet, was born like Mustafa Kemal himself in Salonika, which would not be captured by Greece until the Balkan War of 1912–13.

As Roderick Beaton points out in his welcome biography, *George Seferis: Waiting for the Angel,* even the family name of Greece's first Nobel laureate was not Greek: "*Sefer,* in Turkish, is an Arabic borrowing, related to the word that has come into English as 'safari.' Its principal meanings in both nineteenth century Ottoman and the modern language are: 'Journey, voyage, campaign, state of war.'" The appropriateness of this name to the poet becomes increasingly apparent as you read.

He was born Yiorgos Seferiades, but would shorten his *nom de plume* later on for purposes of self-protection. His father, Stelios, was a lawyer and poet, a formidable, often tyrannical figure in George's life, while his mother, Despo, appears to have been a source of emotional warmth, though weakened by ill health. The family lived at first in prosperous circumstances, wintering in Smyrna and spending summers at the seaside village called Skala. All his life Seferis would remember those idylls and the "wonderful, vernacular Greek" of Skala's fishermen and villagers, as well as his grandmother's nearby house with its massive plane tree in the yard. The oriental plane tree, a relative of our sycamore, is a great presence in Mediterranean villages, often the site of a cistern or fountain, a source of shade in summer heat, a gathering place. I can well imagine the power such a tree and the nearby sea exerted over Seferis's dreams. But he would lose that life and nearly everything Skala had meant to him, leaving one of the deepest wounds of his life.

In 1914, perhaps for career advancement, perhaps sensing more trouble in the Balkans and Asia Minor, Stelios moved his family to Athens, where his closeness to Venizelos would procure him a professorship in law. He sounds in part like one of those frustrated men who force frustration upon their sons, and George would take the brunt of it. Though like his father he had an obvious artistic sensibility, George was compelled to study law in Paris (1918–24) and would eventually have a career in the Foreign Service, starting in the press office and rising through sheer persistence and hard work to become ambassador to Britain in 1957. One way to view Seferis's life is to see him as the artist trapped in a conventional job; it was a source of conflict for him, just as his father's interfering ways had been. But Seferis was good at the work, sometimes clinging to its precarious financial remuneration through cycles of vicious competition from superiors, not to mention precipitous changes of government, World War II, the Greek Civil War and the troubles in Cyprus.

Seferis was a survivor; he learned a tactical circumspection and more than once found himself in the employ of people he despised. Greece's political upheavals were personal to him, starting especially with the Catastrophe of 1922. While the monarchy had maintained a neutral stance in World War I out of loyalty to Germany, the Venizelist government aligned itself with Britain, and as a result of post-war treaties Greece found itself with a foothold once again in Asia Minor. The army overreached, conquering Turkish territory deep inland just as Mustafa Kemal, emboldened by the eradication of the Ottoman Empire, raised his own nationalist army and pushed the Greeks back to the sea. Smyrna burned, and Seferis would not see his childhood home again until a brief visit in 1950.

&

The Beaton biography is very good at outlining such events, proving useful as much to students of modern history as to lovers of Seferis's poetry. The poet's life in this context is a story of endurance and alienation from self—by his father's domination, the loss of Smyrna, a career that often made it necessary to conceal even his love life with a succession of women, then dictatorship, war, exile, and the post-war pursuit of stable government. Yet Seferis survived all this, and the lyrical anguish of the poetry is his testament. Despite the many setbacks of his life, Seferis triumphed as an artist, sometimes remarking bitterly about the price he had to pay.

Henry Miller, who met Seferis in 1939, would call him "more Asiatic than any of the Greeks I met" and "a cross between bull and panther by nature." The poet suited Miller's enthusiasm for the physical and intellectual exuberance of Greece. "His curiosity is insatiable, his knowledge vast and varied. After entertaining me with a selection of the most up to date jazz numbers he wanted to know if I should like to hear more exotic music of which he had an interesting variety."

Miller intuited much, but could not have known the whole picture. As a poet, Seferis in the thirties had relinquished the Symbolist density of his early work and, without quite letting go of Surrealism, had found his mature voice in the remarkable sequence called *Mythistórema,* twenty-four free verse lyrics corresponding to the books of an Homeric epic. It is a poem of both myth and history (the title is the Greek word for a novel), braiding voyages like those of Odysseus and the Argonauts in a modern psychic journey, often expressing his private longing and despair. Before meeting Miller, Seferis had also endured being posted to a consulate in Albania, which separated him from the married woman he loved, who would eventually become his wife, Maró; this desolate assignment had given him more fodder for poetry, including "Epiphany, 1937":

> I've held onto my life held onto my life travelling
> among the yellow trees under the driven rain
> on silent slopes loaded with beech leaves
> no fire on their summits; it grows dark.

Miller did not seem to care much that his friend was now forced to work under the dictatorship of Ioannis Metaxas, his poems expressing revulsion in secretive terms. Seferis was by most accounts good company, but the work of the thirties is full of sorrow at all kinds of oppression. One of his earlier poems, "The Cistern," arose from a euphemism he had devised with a lover, Loukia Fotopoulou, for their private assignations, and he would allude to secret waters again in *Mythistórema:*

> The life they gave us to live, we lived.
> Sorrow for those who wait with such patience
> lost in black laurel beneath the heavy plane-trees
> and those alone who speak to cisterns and wells
> and drown in circles of the voice.

A poet of water as much as earth, Seferis offered both solace and grief in moments of physical presence. He had become a poet of alter-egos, personae such as "Mathios Paskalis" and "Stratis the Seafarer." His poems were alive to the vital presence of Aeschylus as well as the Modernists—an intellectual breadth akin to Cavafy's. Yet like Cavafy he could speak of the personal, as in this untitled fragment:

> This body that hoped like a branch to blossom
> and bear fruit, to become a flute in the frost
> imagination has plunged into a noisy bee-hive
> so musical time may come and torment it.

There is the desire for escape reminiscent of Keats, Yeats and Frost, and a corresponding desire to live plainly in the world, a desire for peace he would too often be denied.

 è&

In the fall of 1946, between postings, Seferis and Maró enjoyed some weeks of unemployment on the island of Poros. In the early years of their marriage they had witnessed the first wave of the German invasion, escaping with the government in exile to Crete, Egypt and South Africa while many of their loved ones lived under the Occupation. Then came the first bloody spasms of the Civil War as former guerilla factions, both leftist and rightist, vied for power with "official" Greece, itself a frag-mented political entity. He would recall the house on Poros, which gave him "for the first time in many years, the feeling of a solid building rather than of a temporary tent." One October Sunday he wrote in his journal. "I woke up . . . with dreams that filled me with joy. I think that since the summer of '40 all my dreams have been public nightmares." The next day he recorded, "In the morning I rowed for an hour and a half, walked for two hours, and, on returning, the sun shining high, I swam. In the afternoon I slept. *My self* has come *out*" (trans. Athan Anagnostopoulos).

On Poros Seferis composed with relative speed one of his most challenging poems, *Thrush,* named for the wreck of "a small naval supply ship, that had been scuttled at the time of the German invasion." In some ways the poem is the closest thing he would write to the method and manner of Eliot, with its mysterious, fragmentary dialogue and allusive range. But its dreamscape reminds me as much of Cocteau's ancient figures marooned in modernity, speaking like ghosts or half-realized human beings. The house becomes a personal symbol for Seferis, harkening back to childhood in Smyrna. Here the statues so emblematic of Greek identity are phantoms of a shat-tered and shattering present.

As early as "The Cistern" he had been obsessed with these presences and absences, and in his most famous poem of the thirties, "The King of Asine," he had opened a fragment of Homer into a haunting meditation:

> . . . or perhaps no, nothing remains but the weight
> the nostalgia for the weight of a living being
> where we the ungrounded ones now abide. . . .

The vividness and physicality of his poetry foundered from the start on existential disquiet.

In his "Letter" on *Thrush* (trans. Rex Warner and Th. Frangopoulos, for a volume of Seferis's essays, *On the Greek Style,* 1966) he would write of the past in a manner similar to Eliot's:

> I think of Aeschylus not as the Titan or the Cyclops that people sometimes want to see him as, but as a man of feeling and expressing himself close beside us, accepting or reacting to the natural elements just as we all do.

Yet his mind seems even more deeply invaded by the past than Eliot's was, and this is surely due to Seferis's language and landscape. As much as the painful journey was his life's pattern, he was more a poet of place. One can see him thinking along these lines in the essay "Cavafy and Eliot—A Comparison":

> But Eliot comes from a rootless place, a place without a past. He feels strongly how paper-thin, how groundless, how unreal and anarchic is, in fact, the order offered by the mechanical civilization of today, his inheritance of material good. He is aware of the drying up of the sources of inspiration.

Seferis had known Eliot's work since his first posting to London in the early thirties, and had translated much of it into Greek. But just as his own Modernist sensibility was formed through acquaintance with French writers before he had learned adequate English to take in Eliot, his conflicted Hellenism and his bureaucratic profession gave him his own individual stance toward history. To some extent, Seferis's cultural background was closer to that of the Alexandrian master:

> Cavafy is not burdened by the absence of a tradition. On the contrary, what he feels is the dead weight of a tradition which is thousands of years old and which he has done nothing to

acquire, since he "carries in him" this "glorious" literate tradition of the Greeks. He is the solitary of an extreme period of Hellenism, the period of the twentieth century.

Seferis is the poet of that Hellenism in crisis, thwarted less by secrets of sexuality, as Cavafy was, than by a more general division of personal and public selves.

It may be significant that of the three poets Seferis is the one who wrote the most eloquent poems against war, though one could argue than an anti-war position is implicit in much that Cavafy produced. I have in mind two great poems from Seferis's *Logbook III,* the volume that expressed his strong feelings about Cyprus. The first of these, "Helen," derives from Euripides's withering revision of Homeric myth—a version in which Helen never went to Troy and the great war was fought for nothing but a phantom. The speaker, one of the Greek soldiers, finds it hard to fathom that "so much pain, so much life / went into the abyss / for an empty nightgown for a Helen." The second anti-war poem I'm thinking of is "Memory I," which begins,

> And I with only a reed in my hands;
> the night was deserted the moon on the wane
> and earth gave off a smell of the last rain.
> I whispered: memory wherever you touch it hurts,
> heaven is shrunken, the sea does not exist,
> what they kill by day they cart to dump behind a ridge.
>
> My fingers played forgetfully with this pipe
> an old shepherd gave me when I said good evening;
> the others have erased each sort of greeting;
> they wake, they shave and start the daily killing
> as one prunes or operates, methodical, passionless;
> pain's as dead as Patroclus and no one errs.

The rage in Seferis is not quite that of Yeats, and Beaton rightly reminds us that, faced with political outrage, he was as suspicious of the *poète engagé* as he was of the ivory tower. Seferis had too much integrity to diminish his art by scoring easy political points. He was not by nature a political animal, though he was by circumstances caught up in political events. The last two crises of his life—the Cyprus issue and the dictatorship of 1967–74—were crises of his nation.

ᔢ

Through his friendships with writers outside Greece and new translations of his work, Seferis became increasingly a public personage. As ambassador to Great Britain he at last had the opportunity to converse with Eliot, who agreed that Seferis was not his literary twin. In a diary (trans. Edmund and Mary Keeley) Seferis detailed his conversations with the elder poet, including Eliot's well-known admonition to be patient with one's job, "because I believe that a great part of poetic creation is unconscious and that there should be times when other things absorb you." Talk of the war years led the men to another illuminating exchange:

> —During the heavy bombing of Crete, I said, I felt best out in the garden reciting old poems with an old villager who remembered them.
> —What about the young ones? Don't they remember them?
> —Much less so.
> —That's how it is; education kills poetry.

Both men understood that powerful aspects of their art were deadened by analysis; both were uncomfortably situated between populists and the critics—they shared that at least. Seferis made much of the *Erotókritos,* the popular epic of sixteenth-century Crete, which he had heard recited by servants in his childhood. He also adored the self-taught General Makriyannis, whose nineteenth-century autobiography became a foundational work in demotic Greek, and he praised the primitive paintings of Theóphilos. These tastes irritated the intelligentsia, while some of his more difficult poetry alienated a larger reading public. It was only through the tireless promotion of friends like George Katsimbalis (Henry Miller's "Colossus") and George Savidis that Seferis's reputation was established. Yet when Savidis took him on a stroll through the Plaka in 1960 so he could hear jukeboxes blaring his lines transformed into popular songs, Seferis was not entirely pleased. A private love poem of his early years, "Denial," would take on, especially under the Colonels, the unexpected stature of an anthem of liberation:

> With what heart, what sighing
> what desire and what passion
> we took up our life: delusion!
> So we changed our life.

❧

When one has loved a poet for many years, one awaits a biography with mixed feelings, hungry for knowledge of the life, but fearful of finding that life diminished by the facts. Roderick Beaton's biography does not diminish the life, but tells it simply and eloquently in a lucid historical context. Beaton is especially good on the forms and backgrounds of the poems. His book is an enrichment.

I do have quibbles. On several occasions Beaton paraphrases when he ought to quote, so we get no samples of the "louche doggerel" and pornographic limericks to which Seferis treated friends in his letters. The life was often melancholy, but Seferis could apparently be quite funny and I'd have liked a stronger dose of his humor. We do get bits of his more rueful wit, of course, like this from 1926: "On 22 August, the unloved dictatorship of General Pangalos was ousted by a *coup d'état.* George noted in his diary: 'here, a dictatorship collapsed the other day . . . , almost silently, like a pile of straw.'" We get grievances and griefs, from his father's strictness to his younger brother's sad death in California, but could use a tad more detail about the man so richly beloved by his close friends.

Still, Beaton's book is thorough in its scholarship and graceful in its style, and in an age of bloated biographies it feels positively economical, weighing in at just over five hundred pages, including copious back matter. Perhaps at the end the narrative is rushed; Seferis hardly had time to enjoy his fame in retirement before the 1967 coup, and Beaton hastens through these years more than he might. I wish he had given further discussion of Seferis's cramped political position, his subdued but forceful denunciation of dictatorship and the way his funeral in 1971 became a rousing public protest in Athens.